PRAISE
JOURNEY WELL, YOU ARE <u>MORE</u> THAN ENOUGH

"Byron & Mariah Edgington have skillfully co-authored *Journey Well, You Are <u>More</u> Than Enough*. This is a manual for self-healing and reflective introspection that goes beyond the words on the page and talks directly to you. The book is overflowing with intimate examples of vulnerability that reveal lessons of life. They go beyond the page by making sure the reader has actionable practice activities to bring those lessons home. Byron safely flies us through perilous moments while Mariah nurses us through our tendency to criticize and shame ourselves. Many guest contributors add depth and variety to the experience. The reader is left with a plan....to Journey Well!"

—Ashok Bhattacharya MD, FRCP(C) author of *Deep Fried Nerves*

"This uplifting, affirming book arrives at a perfect time. *Journey Well, You Are <u>More</u> Than Enough* is a must read for anyone needing a boost of positive energy, and those who know in their heart there's a better way. If you want to feel better about yourself, your identity, and your life purpose, read this book!"

—Jim Obergefell, author with Debbie Cenziper of *Love Wins, The Lovers and Lawyers Who Fought the Landmark Case For Marriage Equality*

"Mariah and Byron write beautifully! I felt as if I were having a conversation with a friend as I read *Journey Well*. There were so many thought provoking, impactful ideas presented in an easy to understand manner. The actionable steps and chapter wrap-ups are brilliant! The activities have really made an impact on me. I can see myself rereading the book again and again, gaining more insights each time!"

—Nancy Barrows M.S. CCC-SLP, Educator

"Byron and Mariah are extremely professional people. It is an honor and privilege to work with them. They are making this world a better place, and people definitely want to check out this book. Being an author, I can tell you that you don't want to miss this book. They are two incredibly kind souls who are moving this world forward through a path of love."

—Rachel Beck is a rising voice in the movement of women's storytelling, and the author of *Finding Your Way When Life Changes Your Plans: A Memoir of Adoption, Loss of Motherhood and Remembering Home*

"I have nothing but praise for Byron and Mariah for their inspiring, elevating book. *Journey Well* releases the heart and encompasses the strength and power of the Universe. I cannot praise this awesome book enough."

—Simon Lever, Featured Contributor to Bizcatalyst360, author *A Beacon Of Positivity, Spreading Optimism, Kindness, and Empathy*

"This book is beautifully and masterfully written from the heart. Its brilliant authors, Mariah and Byron Edgington, eloquently share very important yet often overlooked concepts to empower you, its reader, to *Journey Well* through life. You will come away knowing that you are not only enough, but indeed, you are more than enough. The experts who are highlighted throughout lend much credibility and insight into the multiplicity of skills and techniques you will learn, and that you are gently guided to incorporate into your everyday, sacred life journey."

—Char Murphy ~ Attorney, and Author of *Unshakeable Power: Through Seasons of the Soul*

"*Journey Well, You are More than Enough* by Byron and Mariah Edgington offers a rich, delicious banquet of ideas, inspiration, and wisdom gleaned from the experiences of the authors and contributing writers for living a more fulfilling life in thought and deed. This wonderful book provides meaningful, practical guidance for shifting your mindset to one of gratitude and positivity, ways to create boundaries in our often-distracted daily life, the encouragement to envision an abundant life, and so much more. A thorough guidebook complete with inspiring encouragement, real stories, and practical steps you can take each day, *Journey Well* extends a helping hand to anyone who is navigating troubling times and wants to experience the anchored place of knowing you are more than enough to live well. I heartily recommend this book to all who would appreciate a 3D roadmap for how to live life in wellness and with love."

—Laura Staley Ph.D. Founder, Cherish Your World, Author of *Abundant Heart: Thoughts on Healing, Loving and Living Free, Live Inspired, Let Go Courageously, and the Cherish Your World Gift Book of 100 Tips to Enhance Your Home and Life*

JOURNEY WELL

YOU ARE <u>MORE</u> THAN ENOUGH

JOURNEY WELL

YOU ARE <u>MORE</u> THAN ENOUGH

~

(Re)Discover Your Passion, Purpose, And Love of Yourself & Life

MARIAH EDGINGTON BSN, RN
BYRON EDGINGTON ATP, CRMI

The SkyWriter Press
IOWA CITY

Identifiers:
Library of Congress Control Number: 2022901276
ISBN: 979-8-9854920-4-0 (Paperback) | ISBN: 979-8-9854920-1-9 (Hardcover)
Journey Well You Are <u>More</u> Than Enough// Mariah Edgington, Byron Edgington
First Edition

Book design by: Jeremy Taylor: Instagram.com/jeremy.taylor.ny
Published by The SkyWriter Press in the United States of America
The SkyWriter Press
281 Danielle Street
Iowa City Iowa 52245

www.mariahedgington.com | www.journeywellYAMTE.com | www.byronedgington.com

*Disclaimer: We offer no professional, psychological, mental health, or medical advice. We recognize that people have experienced terrible events in their history, tragedies that haunt them for the rest of their lives. We would never make light of those things or claim that *Journey Well* ignores those deeply damaging events. Please seek professional help. We include a list of resources and further study.

DEDICATION

We salute those who believed in this book, and the *Journey Well* message, to make the world a better, brighter, gentler place by simply calling back the golden values and directives of childhood: To treat others as we wish to be treated; to always be kind; to love each other; to see the astounding power and dignity in everyone; and to honor each person's personal, emotional, and spiritual boundaries.

To our children and grandchildren and beyond, please read this book with a full heart and a generous spirit. Know that we love you, and that we want for you only the kind of world we envision on these pages. There's a better, brighter world waiting, and if we've done nothing else with this book, we've affirmed your birthright to it. Go find it, take care of each other, never be afraid to give and get love, and always go first. Lastly, *Journey Well, You Are More Than Enough.*

"*The quality of your life is a direct reflection of the quality of the choices you make.*"

—MARIAH EDGINGTON

"*The journey of life can change us in ways we never anticipated. We have the ability to raise ourselves up with every decision we make.*"

—BYRON EDGINGTON

TABLE OF CONTENTS

You've believed for a long time that there's a better life.

That you deserve to live in a brighter, gentler world.

That you're a valuable person deserving of respect.

That you have a unique gift to share.

Personal Journey—Ahmad Imam

You sense that mistakes are only lessons.

That your missteps have brought you here.

That humanizing your mistakes brings serenity.

Personal Journey—TM

You recognize the value of your life experience.

You know it's been an amazing journey.

Reperceiving your life starts today.

Your journey will be energizing and invigorating.

Personal Journey—Kim Calvert

Your values are your gift to the rest of us.

Claiming those values brings you dignity.

It shows the world you're to be treated with respect.

That your paradigms must be examined.

Personal Journey—Cory Warfield

≋ You know the words you use are important.

≋ Your words are the image you transmit to the world.

≋ Your words determine who you associate with.

≋ Your words create the better world you imagine.

Personal Journey—Rachel Beck

≋ Boundaries create and project your value.

≋ Boundaries don't reject others, they embrace you.

≋ You observe the boundaries of others as well.

Personal Journey—Diane Wyzga

≋ You know that self-care is not self-ish.

≋ That self-care is claiming your own self worth.

≋ You know that self-care has no end point.

≋ That self-care is a life affirming exercise.

Personal Journey—Laura Staley Ph.D.

≋ You know that fire energizes, warms, comforts, and destroys.

≋ That burning your baggage is caring for yourself.

≋ That burning your baggage destroys what holds you back.

Personal Journey—Brad Burchnell

≋ You know that all you have you imagined into your life.

≋ You're ready to imagine the amazing life you know you deserve.

≋ You're ready to visioneer that life in specific, colorful detail.

Personal Journey—Ali & Dennis Pitocco

≋ You understand Abundance, Awareness, Choice, and Decision.

≋ You know the world must become better and brighter.

≋ You're eager to see that, and to help it happen.

Personal Journey—Whitney Johnson

≋ You know your thoughts become your reality.

≋ You believe that positive is better than negative.

≋ You've believed for a long time that your ideas are amazing.

Personal Journey—Zen Benefiel & Dr. Melissa Hughes Ph.D.

You've done the hard work, imagined the amazing new life for yourself, that better, brighter day you always knew was there for you. Celebrate it! Revel in it! You deserve it, and we're thrilled for you as you Journey Well, because You Are <u>More</u> Than Enough.

Now it's time to share this amazing new you, your unique gift, and the story of your journey with others. As we write, Giving = Receiving, pay it forward, and be prepared to receive in abundant measure. Thank you for finding us, for being who you are, for sharing your story with us, and for your dedication. And thank you for sharing your gift.

FOREWORD

A bundance. Awareness. Choice. Decisions. Four common words that figure heavily in this book. We live in a world of abundance. We must become aware of that. What we do with that understanding is a choice. Our decisions around that choice can create our abundant lives.

You know there's a better, brighter, more abundant life waiting for you. Do you have the courage to create it? If you do, *Journey Well, You Are More Than Enough* gives you guidance, power, and permission.

We believe there's an abiding power in your life that calls you to do that. This energy—the term we use is, 'Universe —is bigger, more pervasive, and more directive than you can imagine. It's available to you and to all of us for the task ahead, and if we're to live full and abundant lives, we must embrace it. We believe this universal energy is in all of us, that it IS us.

PERSONAL JOURNEY
CATHY GRIFFIN

"I help women; tired, burnt-out, fed-up women to confidently design their own compelling future, personal purpose, business clarity, mindset tools."

Cathy Griffin is a Mindset Coach and rockstar. After a tumultuous past, she made the choice to craft the future she envisioned. Cathy is writing a book about her life, so stay tuned. It will be valuable reading, and a road map for many others struggling to claim their value.

~

I've lived my life bouncing back from circumstance after circumstance. I don't want to live like that anymore. Today, I want to live by creating and choosing what I want my future to look like. That's the part about reperceiving yourself. I've made it my business to expand my thinking and spiritual horizons. I'm not here to ascribe anybody with a particular belief. But once I learned I can harness mindset, and expand my thinking, then I can design the future I choose. A future that I truly love. I believed the wrong people on the way up, so that takes some undoing to let go of that and to reperceive yourself.

My life to that point had been a litany of consequences and tragedy. I couldn't tie it all together, like what good is my life? How can I help people with this hodgepodge of crap? At 16 I had a baby boy out of wedlock. I became a nurse at my father's insistence because they didn't know what else to do with me. I went straight to New Orleans from nursing school. When I got bored with the nurses I worked with, I took myself down to the French Quarter, and promptly met the wrong crowd. I became an alcoholic and a drug addict. After five years, I sat straight up in bed, at midnight, and I heard a voice that told me *you will die if you stay here.* I was over 30 when I got sober, when I was pregnant with my daughter. I didn't keep up my nursing license, so when I went to get it renewed all my arrests showed up, and I had to jump through hoops.

I got pregnant at 36, with my son D, and then he died March 21st 2011, a teen suicide.

A year and a half before that, I'd gotten a phone call, and a man said, "I'm looking for Cathy Griffin. My name's M. I think you're my mother." The last time I saw him, thirty-five years before, he was five days old. So, M and D got to meet each other, and knew each other as brothers before D died. But I couldn't understand — why did I find one son, and then lose another one?

As a healthcare executive I was making 105 thousand dollars a year plus 20 to 30 K in bonuses, because I always hit the management goals. Then one morning when I came to work, I was let go from my corporate nursing job with no severance, no notice, and with a flawless employment file. I thought, why do these things happen to me? I'd been study-ing some Bob Proctor, mindset training. Since then, I've been on this journey of focused mindset improvement.

My story isn't wholly about sobriety. It's about over-coming circumstances. Before a person even asks for help, you must be *willing* to ask for help. I've heard it referred to as a key in your pocket. That bit of willingness was and is the key to the beginning of faith and hope. For me, willing-ness came at a price. But whether it's having my first-born when I was 16, losing a son 11 years ago, recovering from alcohol and drug addiction, from a hopeless state of mind, every *ask* for help. For some reason, every ask for help was preceded by what I call a lower bottom. I can't say *rebuild* my life, but build a *new* life, I didn't want to rebuild the old one.

Honesty is huge. If I'm going to ask for help, I must be honest enough to say whatever I'm doing over here on my own is not working. I think that's hard for smart people. We want to figure it all out. But I needed to just listen and be open minded and willing to say OK, and willing to fol-low directions.

I've been hardheaded, stubborn. If you reperceive those attributes, it's what kept me alive. I discovered a seedy side of New Orleans and ended up hanging out with people I shouldn't have. But I survived that. So, persistence and re-silience are what kept me alive. But if you keep relying on that, and don't learn how to have a vision for your future, then you're constantly battered around by whatever life tosses your way. I can't stop tragedy like losing my 16-year-old boy to suicide. I'd do anything to stop that, but I can't. Something in his brain went wrong, and told him a lie, and he believed it. But if you're only using your survival instincts, you're only reacting to circumstance and just waiting for stuff to happen. Some people say God's will is going to happen. They just sit and wait for what comes next in their life. I don't agree with that. Maybe whatever is happening is because you haven't had the vision to go after the dream God planted in your head or in your heart. That's a cop out. That's lazy to me.

When you add awareness to those attributes you can tie all that up in a much prettier bundle. Once I got sober, I learned I had all this range of emotions in between extreme highs and passed out. I had to learn how to manage daily life. I didn't know how to plan for my future, all I knew was how to survive. You cannot be creative in those moments. By this time, as a sober single parent, all I was doing was putting food on the table and fighting to stay on society's hamster wheel. Determination, confidence, resilience and Pissed-Off-Edness were my superpowers. As a woman, if you gather up all your attributes, you can create the kind of future that truly lights you up and will serve your goals and serve others.

If my faith is constant, the universe always has my back. You know, God got you through 100% of your bad days so far, so what makes you think he's not going to get you through the next one?

As far as achieving C- level goals, some days I must remind myself that, more than ever, I am <u>More</u> than enough. If you do any kind of self-analysis, it becomes apparent that there's something greater than you. You become more self-aware of your own limitations and learn how to focus on your inner strengths. However, if you're not honest with yourself, the only person you are enabling is you. Self-enabling. I've known people who believe their own lies. I do not wish to be one of them.

I'd say that going through a 12-step program to get sober is what initially made me spiritually centered. To believe in something much greater, and eventually myself. The steps are not religion. This is what gave me the tools to believe in something. They take you through a self-analysis — they call it a fearless moral inventory — that says you don't regret the past, but you don't shut the door on it either. How else is a person going to save themselves if they're not aware of what they need to change, then use mindset resources, and become aware of their own amazing attributes and unlimited potential?

INTRODUCTION

JOURNEY WELL

HAS FOUND YOU

"This book arrived by way of the promoters of
human potential and dignity past and present."
—MARIAH EDGINGTON

Y ou've found *Journey Well, You Are More Than Enough.*
Or *Journey Well* has found you. Either way, we welcome
you to a book that will raise you up as high as you deserve
to be, and where you belong. *Journey Well* affirms your emerging
belief that a better way, a better world, is not only possible for you,
it's already here. Now, today, in these strange and disruptive times,
it's up to all of us to recognize this amazing new opportunity, to
promote it, and to celebrate it. It's your turn, and we're honored to
help you in this exciting time. Exciting because it's wholly possible,
and because you have the choice to make it happen. Making choic-

1

es underlies and energizes every aspect of your journey. It's hard work, but it's worth everything you give to it.

Here's the *most* exciting and "energizing" part: The choice is available to you to make the changes needed in your world right now. But you can only use this energy if you know its value, and your own, and only when you trust in its provenance. As poet William Blake wrote, *"What seems to be, is, to those whom it seems to be."* Imagining this new world, this brighter life for yourself and others is already here, if only you believe it is. As Kim Calvert of Dynamite Lifestyle says, "Believe in your ability to create an abundant lifestyle. You will never go beyond that which you believe."

As a guide to the task, *Journey Well* offers you a message of hope. Hope for bringing gratitude into your daily life, hope for focusing on what's good, and letting go of the negatives and the *cants* that seem to come too easily. Since we're immersed in a world flooded with negative messages on social media and elsewhere, *Journey Well* offers a corrective. Purveyors of poison thrive on our addiction to fear and apprehension. Their dismal negativity can sap your soul. We choose positive, uplifting messages instead, to help you turn your back on that predatory messaging, deciding instead to take this ultimate, soul-satisfying journey called life not just adequately but well. We'll show you that silencing your inner critic is salutary, and possible.

YOU HAVE GREAT VALUE...CLAIM IT

The message is that we must treat ourselves and others with dignity and respect, gratitude and kindness, because, regardless of whether you're a pauper or a prince, you're a vital human being, a member of a tribe marked by great dignity, and meant for great things. You have a precious gift to add to the already abundant world we live in. You have great value. It's time for you to claim it.

Did we feel a bit of apprehension in pushing *Journey Well* and its positive message into the world at this time? Yes, we did. Especially with a waning but still deadly virus stalking the world, and the equally malevolent forces of despair discouraging us from maintaining our positive outlook, we felt the drag and the tethering of negative pressures. This is precisely why *Journey Well, You Are More Than Enough* is important right now, because as we humans have made our way through the hollows of time, hope is often all we've had. But then, as in other equally challenging eras, hope is all we've ever needed. We can do this, and with your help, success is assured.

This statement may sound a bit removed from reality for some readers: We don't believe we wrote this book; we're merely the vessels through which it came to be. The physical product you hold in your hands, the words in front of you issued from the energy of numerous prophets of abundance, the philosophers of hope and prosperity. This book arrived by way of the promoters of human potential and dignity past and present. *Journey Well* is simply a manifestation of the energy that flows around and through us, the Universal force that directs all we do, including the transcribing of words onto pages and then into books.

THE UNIVERSE IS ABUNDANT

Here's the core message of *Journey Well, You Are More Than Enough:* Every one of us is a precious addition to the collective consciousness called humanity. No one in this human family can be left behind, or we're all diminished. We believe we humans sense in our DNA that the universe is abundant, that all the riches that exist are available to us, and that we have an obligation to act on that abundance to the benefit of others. This includes you.

We believe that the only path forward in fully living is in fully giving. Those two words, living and giving, are just one letter apart, so closely aligned that we make no separation between them. Living = Giving. We know this. For us personally, as long as we remember, we've given things away: money, time, and resources. Every time it happens, we notice a curious outcome: The more we give away, the more comes back to us. This seeming contradiction is partly what drives this book.

Giving in such fashion was a bit unsettling for us at first, a little distressing as we freely gave, and then gave more, watching items of our hard-won industry going away, sometimes given to people we hardly knew. We did know they needed those material things more than we did. So, we gave them away. And then, as sure as day follows night, that abundance always returned to us, even richer, and every time. Quite often, the returning item or gift arrived in a different form, something more fitting to us, a manifestation that can only be called grace.

However, our surrender to the impulse for generosity posed its own fascinating necessity: Energy being constant, neither created nor destroyed, for the universe to function properly and to balance out we had to learn to receive. That part has been more difficult than learning to give. But it's equally necessary for a critical balance to emerge. This universal balancing act reinforces our long-held belief that we do not live in a zero-sum world. That there's <u>More</u> than enough for everyone, or it wouldn't be called a world of abundance.

This feeling is true for you, too, or you wouldn't be holding *Journey Well* in your hands. We're guessing you're like us, and like a growing host of people in this quickly shifting time, our giving nature, and our dedication to a better world, starts with an acceptance of this seemingly contradictory tenet: The only way to receive, is to give.

Also, we understand that the journey itself is the true basis of satisfaction. That the gathering of material things, the shiny objects that fill our closets, and garages, and houses, and cities bring us no deep or long-term satisfaction. The ability to look beyond those transitory items, and to journey well driven solely by our hearts, is a rare and precious gift. But it's a gift that can be taught, and also learned. By seeking this new world with open hearts and accepting minds we will find ourselves.

In *Journey Well* you'll read affirming messages, a series of gratifying quotes and citations that you'll relate to in your own daily quest for peace, meaning, and contentment. Many of these quotes you've heard before from our social media posts; many will be new to you. They're positive, uplifting messages, always. They're words that add only good energy, and all are intended to help you journey well.

Following each chapter, we include another gift, that is, personal journeys freely given to us by dear friends to add power and affirmation to our message. To those who contributed to *Journey Well*, our heartfelt thanks and huge loving hugs to all of you. We're humbled by your generosity and your courage.

This is not the typical book of tired aphorisms, or of flowery, poetic dismissals of real and difficult daily challenges. Times are tough, there's no denying that. We never dismiss true human suffering, or the real tragedies that haunt and disrupt people's lives. Our words simply serve as a road map for your personal path into a new and better world, a world we must craft together.

And we *must* craft it together. Like all worthwhile initiatives, *Journey Well* comes with a mandate. We are called to elevate others, and so are you. As our friend Lorena Acosta wrote, *Someone out there, a person you may never know, needs to hear your voice or see-feel your presence. You could be the reason someone decides today is the day they will have the COURAGE to speak up, follow their dream, or make a decision that could be the start to a more fulfilled life.* Lorena is right. Your actions could save a life, either figuratively or literally. This is another reason your power must be acknowledged and embraced.

We also believe that what we read, hear, see, and share are staple items for either the sustenance or the subversion of our souls. It's a choice. Either a diet of positive, generous, and grateful messages as the best way to enrich our spiritual selves, or soul-sapping indulgence in the much too common negativity poisoning our world. This is what we know: The more we feed our minds with positive, uplifting fare the faster our journey toward a better world will be. For that reason, in *Journey Well* we celebrate positive, elevating messages, avoiding those that detract, or diminish.

JOURNEY WELL IS A PILOT LIGHT FOR YOUR OWN REDISCOVERY

In *Journey Well* you'll read several references taken from our past career paths. Mariah was a nurse for many years; I was a pilot. We base many of our observations on the framework of those occupations, work we both dearly loved. Indeed, we never considered it work because our careers allowed us to serve others, and in doing that, we found our bliss. So, consider *Journey Well* a pilot light for your own rediscovery, and a chance to nurse yourself as you deserve.

Last, we believe with all our hearts that seeking the best in each other, and in yourself, will result in a better, richer, more gracious society. Whatever you focus on expands. This maxim works in all directions, in every place, and in every era. Also, as the late Bob

Proctor of Proctor Gallagher Institute said, "If you can hold it in your head, you can hold it in your hand." In other words, if you can imagine something—a new car, new home, a bigger bank account or a gentler new world—you can facilitate its arrival in your life.

MORE THAN ENOUGH, BECAUSE MORE IS UNLIMITED

Let us explain our subtitle: *You Are More Than Enough.* We often hear "you're fine," and "you're okay." People use the simple expression "you are enough." We don't believe that quite says it; we claim that you are More than enough. We're not patronizing you. We're stating an undeniable, readily apparent truth: You are an amazing, beautiful, wonderfully precious human being. The power residing inside you is so immense, so limitless, that when you realize its presence and touch it yourself you'll be astonished, perhaps even a bit reluctant to use your unlimited power. As Shakespeare wrote in Hamlet, *what a piece of work is man, how noble in reason, how infinite in faculty.* He was writing about you.

Let us address our readers who are different. You've heard all your life that you're abnormal, or strange, or that you don't fit in, or that you need to shape up, learn to get along, stop being a problem. What that message really says is *stop being who you are.*

Journey Well is different too. We welcome everyone. We celebrate everyone. It's a tragedy that your difference is shunned, that you're often left outside looking in. We believe the unique and different way you inhabit the world is something to celebrate, something everyone must be able to openly share with the rest of us. We believe we have an obligation to explore, promote, accept, and yes celebrate every human being because everyone carries their own precious piece of this vast and beautiful puzzle we're crafting together.

SELF-DISCOVERY, THE MOST DIFFICULT & PERILOUS
TRIP YOU'LL EVER TAKE

You are a worthy person. Be proud of what you've done, who you are, and the way you're going to use this universal energy. Here's where to start. Imagine setting off on the most important journey of your life. This voyage of self-discovery is to be the most perilous and difficult trip you've ever taken. It's invigorating, gratifying, sometimes terrifying, but always richly rewarding. It's the best journey you'll ever take, and along the way you'll emerge at a place you're happy to call home.

Know this at the outset: You will arrive at that place, you will take great pride in your success, and you are going to journey well. Lest you doubt our qualifications to bring this message to you, we've both had the great benefit of being "wisely wounded" in life, experiencing our own personal tragedies and triumphs along the way. We've both sought professional counseling and psychological conferrals. At times in our own lives, we sought help with daunting problems, issues that brought despair and anguish and drove us to seek help. We share some of those stories with you here.

If something has happened to you, either emotional or physical violence of any kind, issues that conjure thoughts of harming yourself, depleting whatever self-esteem you have, we know from personal experience that asking for help can be your salvation. In another proof of the binary universal—giving is receiving—by reaching out and giving of yourself, you're owning your power. That's what powerful people do. They acknowledge their place in this amazing human family and ask for help.

We hope *Journey Well* fills your need for deeper satisfaction. We hope it gives you a rich, rewarding affirmation: That better, more abundant living is here, it's now, and it's yours. Reading *Journey Well, You Are More Than Enough*, your deep spiritual craving will be affirmed to be real, and true, and yours. Fellow traveler, we welcome you with open arms.

ME/BE.

PERSONAL JOURNEY

AHMAD IMAM

"A Top 10 Influencer to Follow In 2021 | International Man of
Empowerment 2021 | Presenter | Host | Ambassador to the Royal Office UAE |
Social Media Consultant to HNWIs."

I was bullied for being different. Yes, it's true. Throughout my schooling, I was bullied almost daily because I looked different, spoke different, and behaved different. I was a small, skinny, brown-skin immigrant with big glasses and an unkempt afro. I was called names, pushed around, pointed at, and laughed at for simply being different to the average kid. It hurt.... but I internalized the pain.

Every day I'd put on a brave face and pretend it didn't affect me because I was afraid of appearing weak. This continued for over 10 years. One of the saddest things about bullying is that when you get bullied for such a long period of time, you begin to believe other people's opinions of you.

And I must admit...it broke me. My self-worth was destroyed. My confidence was crushed. And my self-esteem was non-existent. I entered a dark place. My opinion of myself was so low that I couldn't even look people in the eye. And...I didn't even want to speak to anyone, because I truly believed I didn't deserve to hold the voice space. After much soul searching, and an introduction to personal development, I was able to overcome this. How? By reminding myself of 4 valuable truths. 1. Bullies are often reflecting their own insecurities. 2. Your value doesn't decrease based on someone's inability to see your worth. 3. You have to be kind to yourself, because how you treat yourself sets the tone for how others treat you. 4. You shouldn't be afraid of being different. You should be afraid of being the same as everyone else.

I used to be ashamed of the fact I was bullied, in fact I hid it for many years, until I came to the realization that it made me who I am. I am now a Presenter, Host, Influencer, and Content Creator.... Being different is now my greatest superpower. If you've ever been bullied, you have a choice to respond in one of 2 ways: 1) You can reflect the same behavior onto others and become a bully or 2) You can spread love and kindness by using your pain to better serve others. I have chosen the second path. Embrace all that you are...and protect it. Because being different is your greatest superpower.

CHAPTER ONE

MISTAKES /
HUMANIZING

FAIL YOUR WAY

TO THE MOON!

"We can all win, even after mistakes, or because of them!"
—BYRON EDGINGTON

During NASA's Apollo program, the lunar spacecraft had a device onboard that was programmed to track the vehicle's exact course to the moon. This mechanism detected errors from the correct course within a few meters. Any time the ship's course diverged, the steering mechanism brought it back, and the three Apollo astronauts continued on their way. Engineers at NASA said they'd "failed their way to the moon." In other words, without the failures, the math-driven device would never have learned how to make corrections.

THERE ARE NO FAILURES, ONLY LESSONS

You haven't made mistakes. You've simply failed your way to a brighter, better life. The baggage you'll unpack doesn't contain your failures. It's packed with lessons. Every misstep along the way steered you back on course. This book is a course correction on your voyage of discovery.

Our contention is that your mistakes have been learning opportunities. To understand this, you need to suspend disbelief for a bit. Most people think the world is waiting for them to fail so the stronger, smarter, or better socially positioned among us can get ahead. When you think you've failed, of course you feel shame. But we don't live in that world. We live in an abundant world, and abundant is just another word for forgiving. We can all win, even after mistakes, or because of them.

Every trip begins with a first step. That first step can be exciting, but it can also be nerve-wracking. No trip worth taking is easy, smooth, or entirely safe. Risk can never be eliminated, only minimized. As much as we try to remove or reduce risks to ourselves, our hearts, our emotions, our feelings, they can never be wholly dismissed. We must always risk a mistake or two, or we'll never move ahead.

In *The Death of Ivan Ilyich*, Tolstoy's main character dies. In his final hours, Ivan Ilyich endures excruciating physical pain. But his emotional pain is worse. Ilyich believes that his life has been dull and ordinary, that he's never discovered who he truly is. He says, "What if my entire life, my entire conscious life, simply was not the real thing?" It's a chilling question, and one reason our mistakes haunt us so much.

It would be the ultimate agony to die believing you never truly lived, far worse than any physical suffering. One thing holding you back from that exploration is fear of making a mistake. By convincing you to stay in your safe, familiar cocoon, that fear keeps you in a predictable and ordinary life. But like an aircraft parked in a hangar, or a boat on dry land, that's not why you're here. You're here to take off and soar. Without risk, your life truly would be *not the real thing.* Fear is also where that damnable inner voice has taken up residence.

Melissa Hughes Ph.D. refers to herself as a "neuroscience geek," albeit one with extensive knowledge of the human brain. Hughes says our brains didn't evolve to think; they evolved to keep us alive and safe. Eons past, when we shared the earth with predators who considered us to be lunch, danger was everywhere. That's when our initial fear response evolved, and it still exists, still kicking in to keep us safe ages later. It's where the negative inner voice comes from with the message that no matter what you do, no matter what your accomplishments, you must keep reaching for a higher branch to escape the angry beast bearing down on you. It's also why mistakes crowd our minds faster and longer than our successes do. It's why the smallest misstep lingers in our minds, while even major success fades away quickly and is forgotten. "Your project won first prize!" lasts a day or two. "You backed into another car" stays for weeks. This is the reason that celebrating your triumphs is so important.

Today's predator is not a feral beast on the savanna, it's in your mind. But it's just as limiting and dangerous to your progress. These days, it's called impostor syndrome, and even the highest achievers among us have a touch of it. There's an excellent TEDx talk given by Dr. Hughes at Wabash College addressing impostor syndrome. It's worth watching.

Here's an example of what can happen when success is assumed, and mistakes are considered unlikely. Recently, Sir Richard Branson rode his Unity capsule to the very edge of space. When the tiny craft dropped from the mothership and fell free, for a small slice of time it was not assured that its engine would ignite, or that the Unity would ride its tongue of fire upward into space. In that short time span fear could have prevailed. It did not. Unity's engine burst to life in a brilliant flag of fire propelling Unity's crew upward. Fear lost that day; our collective preference of hope prevailed. It's not likely that Branson or people like him will ever wonder on their final day if their lives have been *the real thing*. You don't have to be concerned about that either.

We envision *Journey Well, You Are More Than Enough* as your flag of fire, your assumption of success giving you a powerful, uplifting message of hope. It's for you to use to confront the voice of fear that warns you not to make a mistake, and that tries to quench your inner fire. When you leave the old, tethered *you* far behind, you'll fly higher than ever.

Everyone makes mistakes. It's called being human. There's no going back and changing them, they've brought you where you are now. Consider them as lessons learned, a leap forward, and go on.

When mistakes happen, and you hear, *they were right; I am stupid, lazy, ignorant,* your harsh inner critic may scream at you to *sit down, stay in your place, don't make trouble! You'll never amount to anything.* Many people feel this way. You might scream at yourself and think all kinds of angry and demeaning thoughts. But consider this. You wouldn't yell at your child or grandchild that way. Why do that to yourself?

Here's another aviation analogy offering a reason to let go of mistakes and to move forward. Aircraft are designed to be aerodynamic. Look at an aircraft parked at the gate. Notice that just sitting still it appears to be flying. Graceful wings sweep back in pleasing symmetry; cowls, covers, and the leading edges of its wings are smooth and polished to meet the air with no resistance. The slightest gust of wind would lift the airplane off the ground and carry it aloft.

Aircraft are designed and built to be as sleek and aerodynamic as possible to overcome the forces of gravity, weight, drag, and wind resistance.

They were never designed to fly backward. Trying to fly an aircraft backward would result in terribly awkward movements, and the confounding of basic forces. Same graceful wings; same sleek, airworthy design. But an airplane in reverse would never fly. It would succumb to anomalous forces and crash.

We're designed for going forward, just as aircraft are. Think about your car. The rearview mirror is much smaller than the front windshield. That's because going forward is more important than going backward.

OUR ERRORS, AS UNCOMFORTABLE AS THEY FEEL AT THE TIME, OFTEN GUIDE US TO OUR BETTER WORLD

Looking back at past mistakes, missteps, and judgment errors is beneath your dignity, and it impedes your progress. Going over things again, allowing them to manipulate your life, confounds the smooth and polished structures you've crafted since you sanded down your rough edges. It dismisses the brilliant design features that define your life, your ability to hope, to look ahead, and to see each new day as a chance to take off again, with an opportunity to fly ever higher.

As for impostor syndrome, ask yourself why you should be good at a task right out of the box? Were you born knowing how to promote the new product, or play chess? The day you entered the world, could you do advanced math? Of course not. Be gentle with yourself. Many people we consider to be experts, if they're honest, will tell you they've had their own doubts about their ability.

Mistakes are part of the human condition, so in many ways they make you more human. Thus, it's easier for others to empathize with you. It will help you Journey Well.

HERE ARE THREE IMPORTANT POINTS FROM THIS CHAPTER:

★ You didn't make mistakes. You failed your way forward.
★ It takes years of self-reflection to step into your truth.
★ Sometimes when you lose your way, you find YOURSELF.

ACTION STEPS:

≋ Start a gratitude journal. Gratitude journaling is a very effective way to elevate your energy level and raise your spirits.
≋ Our minds believe what we tell them. Tell yourself—in writing—what you're grateful for, and that energy will come back to you.
≋ Write ways you "failed forward" in life.

PERSONAL JOURNEY

TM

TM relates a story that tugged at our hearts, a humanizing tale from its courageous and loving author. TM's story reveals yet another side of the self-care theme we stress in *Journey Well*, an aspect few consider: How self-care fosters stronger families, especially with the ingenious approach TM used as part of the therapy, leaving a journal out for her child to read.

It's difficult enough today with frantic work, plus the Covid virus, and family responsibilities. Throw in a crisis of sexual abuse, and self-care goes from luxury to necessity. Here is TM's story, initialized because of the sensitive nature of the topic.

~

The importance of self-care became profoundly apparent to me following my daughter's disclosure of sibling sexual abuse. As a counselor I would always preach the necessity of self-care regularly to my clients. I quickly realized during our crisis that I certainly did not have the balance right, and I put self-care on the backfoot. It led me to burn out rapidly.

I poured all my energy into my daughter, and all my other family members, leaving little to nothing for myself. It came to a make-or-break point for me when I realized if I continued, I would very quickly drown. I was of no use to anyone. I spent most nights comforting my daughter until the early hours of the morning, and still getting up thinking I could function and continue as normal. I worked 3 days a week, trying to homeschool 5 days a week due to Covid. I had a young baby, and a spouse who had a successful business. We built a beautiful house next door to my in-laws as they were getting older and required some caring responsibilities. This meant I was 45 minutes away from my own family, so didn't have the physical support of them when required.

My spouse had self-care in abundance, attending the gym 5 days a week, golfing at the weekends and other activities. This left very little room for me, and I'll admit I was quite resentful that I did not have the opportunities and felt very restricted and limited. I had to change this, and I did. This was the turning point for me and my family.

The first thing I needed to do was relinquish some responsibilities, to allow myself to breathe and not become so overwhelmed. The first thing I started with was boundaries. You may ask what has that to do with self-care? This is the pinnacle of self-care in my opinion. I was the 'people pleaser,' the rescuer, the person everyone came to if they had a problem. I couldn't do or be that person when I was going through this major trauma. I had to put myself first, something that was alien to me, but eventually liberating. I had to distance myself from others as their negativity brought me right down. I also took an extended break from work. I had to minimize as much responsibility as possible and focus on my priorities.

Covid restricted a lot of the social connections I once had i.e. hobbies like netball etc. I hated walking, but I recognize that was an excuse to keep me demotivated. I started walking the dog in the evenings, even when I had no energy. It was vital to push on through, and I am so glad I did. The time and space alone helped me clear my head and replenish.

Throughout this process I recognized I was being everything for everyone and losing myself in the process, so I also took to journaling. I kept a diary for when I was becoming so overwhelmed to process my feelings. This was very cathartic. I used the journal to communicate with my daughter, leaving it open at times so she could read it. Obviously, I kept it quite censored, but I used it as a platform to communicate what I needed to tell her in an indirect way. She found it difficult talking about the situation, her feelings, the processes etc, so anything I wanted her to know I wrote in there. It also helped me gain much more clarity. It inspired me to do and be more. It helped motivate me and energize me.

I am a firm believer that 'you cannot pour from an empty cup.' First, we must fill our own. It is only by doing that we can be of benefit to anyone. People think self-care is selfish; I call it self-preservation. It doesn't have to be spa trips or shopping malls. It doesn't even have to cost money. A simple bath, dedicating 30 mins to yourself daily, pamper days in the house. I wholeheartedly don't know where I or my family would be if I didn't take a step back and focus on me first, as I am the glue that solidifies us.

CHAPTER TWO

REPERCEPTION /
REVISION

REPERCEPTION:

A NEW WORD, A NEW LIFE

"To be wisely wounded can be the greatest source of your
strength."
—MARIAH EDGINGTON

This is one of the most important chapters in the book. It
has the power to change your life. That is, to reperceive
your life. This chapter offers you simple yet profound al-
ternatives you've needed to attain the level of happiness and contentment you've longed to have, the happiness you know in your
heart you're entitled to.

We've both had the great benefit of being, as Mariah wrote,
"wisely wounded" in life, experiencing our own personal tragedies
and triumphs. There were times when we sought help with daunting problems. We know from personal experience that asking for

help can be your salvation. By reaching out, and making yourself vulnerable, you're owning the power that was stripped from you by self-doubt. Powerful people acknowledge their place in this amazing human family and seek guidance.

WHEN YOU HAVE THE COURAGE TO BE VULNERABLE, AS UNCOMFORTABLE AS IT MAY BE, IT ISN'T A SIGN OF WEAKNESS

Psychologists use the term "unconditional positive regard." It means what it says. We accept and celebrate you, no matter what. We say out loud something that doesn't get said often enough even in private, that you're a beautiful person. You have those positive attributes <u>now</u>, not when you earn as much as your neighbor, not when you finish that degree, not when you lose weight, not when you're being told that you need to _____(fill in the blank) by yourself or those around you. You are <u>More</u> than enough right now.

When our oldest daughter was a child, her favorite TV personality was Mister Rogers. She adored Fred Rogers and his "Neighborhood." We like to think her devotion to the show was because Mister Rogers always said, "I like you just the way you are." That's how we feel about you. Starting now, we want you to say so, too, in order to reperceive things that haunt you from your past. Everyone needs to hear your singular and important message, because it's you, and it's true. So, welcome to *our* neighborhood.

Take note of your past errors, missteps and embarrassments. Go back to your childhood, junior high, high school, college, your early working life, first romantic efforts, first failures with family or relatives. Document your failed classes, blown tests, missed opportunities. Note all those painful things without elaboration. As you place each one on the list, think about your younger self, and reperceive them in a positive way by acknowledging that they helped bring you where you are. Without them you'd be a different person. When you've finished the list, set it aside.

ALLOW US TO LIFT YOU UP

You're a marvelous person who will stride into this glorious party of life with confidence, gracing our grand celebration with an open heart filled with kindness and love, not challenged by those missteps or a nonsense inner voice. Come in now. We welcome you! This is your crowd, my friend, your new, affirming tribe. Allow us to support and praise you and to lift you up.

This is what we do with *Journey Well.* This is your time to shine, to share the splendid gifts within. Your hidden attributes are yearning to be set free. Open yourself to the world. Let us welcome you. We're glad you're here. Cast off those errors and own your value. You are More than enough.

LIFE DEMANDS COURAGE

We've both had life challenges that burdened us, and things that dragged us down. We know your inner critic can be the harshest judge you have, because we've felt that judgment. Arianna Huffington refers to this inner voice as the "obnoxious roommate living in my attic."

We all hear our own inner critic. Its voice is harsh and pervasive, and it must stop. And you have total control over it. As bizarre as it may sound, if you're reading this for the first time, this is absolutely true: The voice inside your head comes from you! It's your own voice you're hearing, so only you can stop it.

When you fail at something, listen and learn what the voice sounds like. What elicits the judgmental nagging? Why is the harsh response so corrosive? Does the voice know a long-held secret you're afraid might get out? Does it remind you of yourself judging others? Is this what you allow others to say to you? This is reperception as well.

Each time you notice a useless message from your abusive attic cackler, we want you to celebrate the fact that you recognized it as injurious! This, too, is reperception. For our own examples, here is Mariah's story.

When I was a carefree six-year-old, I climbed my grandparents' thirty-foot-high barn. My family saw me up there waving, smiling, calling down to them, and they were horrified. The child everybody knew "had to be watched every minute" had once again escaped and was perched on top of the barn! I had no idea at the time that my behavior had already branded me as a brat who was out of control and not to be trusted. Reperceiving this today, I see that even then I was trying to escape the confines of my circumscribed life, trying to climb higher. But the label remains.

THE HARDEST PERSON TO GET TO KNOW IS YOURSELF

It takes being vulnerable to explore what awakens your inner critic. It's like peeling an onion, another activity that can make you cry. It's hard feeling so exposed, but it's how you get to know yourself. As we began some intense introspection years ago, we found the hardest person to get to know was ourselves!

You understand that there's a new world waiting to be born, a new world welcoming you with arms wide or *Journey Well* would not have found you. Instead of harsh, judgmental cries, we're saying, "we thought you'd never get here," and "welcome dear friend!" Being human is being vulnerable. Showing up every day as yourself is the bravest thing you may ever do.

As this bright new world struggles into being, the pain and disruption tell you to let go of your haunting past and to dismiss the things you cannot change, because they drag you back to a more comfortable state—even if that prior condition was terribly dissatisfying or unsafe. Positive, self-affirming thoughts will help you reperceive things in every case. As Louise Hay wrote, "you wouldn't search last night's garbage to make today's meal." None of us want to go backward. We can't do that anyway.

We know there's no going back. New attitudes and new worlds crying to be born cannot be denied. A brighter future is coming for you. When you release your missteps, dismiss the guilt, the blame, and the shame that have tethered you, you'll understand what it's like to journey well.

REPERCEPTION: CHANGE WHAT YOU SEE
TO WHAT YOU WISH TO BE

Recall something right now that, at the time, was shameful and embarrassing. You failed a big test; you were fired; your best friend betrayed you. Did the long-term outcome put you in a better place? This is the power of reperception. It often changes things in your past to positive, better outcomes for you. The events will always be part of who you are, and you're an amazing person today, so your past played a part in that.

We left long-term relationships that were not fulfilling. Doing that, we caused pain to several people. We'd sought a better life for ourselves, when on the surface it appeared we already had perfect lives. Our choice shocked friends and family, causing some to abandon our lengthy friendships. Our choice revealed a truth we'd hidden even from ourselves far too long. We were unhappy in "perfect relationships." Leaving them was good for us but threatening to others.

RELEASE ALL PAST HURTS AND MISSED OPPORTUNITIES, AND EXPRESS GRATITUDE FOR THE NOW

No matter what you did yesterday, the day before, or last year, you can't alter it physically, regardless of your actions today. But reperceiving those things and doing so with self-love frees you from the tether that holds you back.

This is the core of reperception. When you subscribe to the idea that you can't change the past or live in the future today, that you live your life in the present tense, you release all the past hurts and missed opportunities and express gratitude for the now. If this sounds like our way to excuse actions from years past, think of it this way: Just as ours have, all the decisions you made in your past have brought you to this point. They've taught you valuable lessons about what life is at its core, and who you are at your most basic self.

THE BERLIN WALL & REPERCEPTION

The Berlin Wall was toppled in 1989. After the wall fell, interesting stories emerged from both sides, from those who'd lived in the western sector and from those in the east. It became apparent that neither side understood exactly what the wall meant. Westerners thought it kept people from escaping East Berlin. Easterners thought it kept westerners out of their communist Eden. After the wall fell, both sides understood that the real wall was never concrete and iron; the real wall was in their minds.

What's the limiting wall you've built in your mind? It may not be what you think. And it is <u>exactly</u> what you think. In the guidebook, we offer an exercise for you to list any limiting beliefs you hold, your personal Berlin Wall. Socrates said an unexamined life isn't worth living. We believe that to be true.

Examining yourself by reperceiving past events and exposing mental walls is a bold, valuable exercise for you to celebrate.

Reperception opens up vast new realms of possibility. It gives you a chance to see the entirety of your life in a better and a brighter light. Going forward, you can reperceive whatever you now imagine and the way your life will evolve. This ability, coupled with the change in attitude and mindset, will make the clouds and mist dissipate in front of you as the better, brighter life comes into view. Perceive your future as if it's here now, just the way you wish it to be.

IF YOU CAN IMAGINE IT, YOU CAN HAVE IT

So, remember that word: Reperception. It's a way to look at the past in a more positive light and to make peace with it. Too often, simple appearances deceive you, especially if your default is to conjure negative, bitter, or disappointing things that come your way. Viewing them through the clear lens of reperception changes how they register in your mind. That change will raise you to a higher level. It will help you *Journey Well.*

HERE ARE THREE IMPORTANT POINTS FROM THIS CHAPTER:

★ Stop the inner critic immediately. Congratulate yourself for noticing and substitute a positive affirmation.

★ To reperceive your past, harvest the gems. Leave the junk behind.

★ We all hear an inner critic at times. Its voice is harsh and pervasive, and it has to stop. You have total control over it.

ACTION STEPS:

≋ Become aware of when your inner critic enters your thoughts. Are you tired? Bored? Frustrated?

≋ Have affirmations ready so you can refer to them right away. *I'm a very accomplished person. Let me tell you about my awards. I am More than enough!*

≋ Remind yourself whose voice that is: It's yours!

PERSONAL JOURNEY

KIM CALVERT

"Director of Dynamite Lifestyle Ltd. | Executive Diamond Pin Achiever |
Certified Proctor Gallagher Consultant | 14x Inner Circle Member |
Circle of Excellence Member."

This personal journey was shared with us by Kim Calvert, Executive Officer of Dynamite Lifestyle Ltd. Kim's message from parents and peers was that only by scraping and scratching could she hope to survive. Through hard work and persistence, she built an international, multimillion dollar company that teaches others how to make that mindset change for themselves and to reperceive their lives.

Before, I'd been a poor nurse, an Irish girl with just four pounds twenty to my name. I decided to reperceive things, to change my mindset from lack to abundance. Here is what I discovered.

Our job, I believe, is to change our visions and to tap into our higher levels of that. We do that by reperceiving what we used to see, focusing our minds on the positive, on what is good, and really that comes back to love. Before, I didn't love myself. So first, I believe we need to love ourselves fully before we can love others. Before we can help others find abundance, we've got to first accept *our* abundance. It's a mindset change including reperception. I believe that our journey has many different levels, many different destinies that we're all going to experience, and I don't believe that once you've got a certain amount of money, or achieved a high level, that's it.

Our thoughts and our feelings put us on different levels of frequencies and vibrations, so we're energy, and we can transmute ourselves into those beautiful, physical things.

Like everybody else, I wanted more abundance in my life, I also wanted more abundance in finances, and when I read and studied mindset and reperception, it made me realize that often what we're really spending is our thoughts: time and money. That's another reperception.

"Awareness is what really creates abundance."

—KIM CALVERT

A lot of people are living in a world of lack because they're spending their thoughts. That means they're focusing their time thinking about things they don't have. Thinking about things causing doubts, fears, and worries. It's costing them in their bank balance, in their health, in faith, in so many other ways. We must invest our thoughts, and that's something I've personally experienced. I believe I'm God's highest form of creation, and me becoming who

I am is sharing my abundance with others, because I can't give what I haven't got.

I think we all have been chosen for different purposes. I believe my destiny is to share this incredible awareness with others, and reperception and awareness are what really create abundance. The more aware we become, the greater our life is. I had to love *me* first, then I had to *be* me, and I had to be free to be me. And throughout this journey, I have to know who "me" is. I believe that's a piece of work that everybody must do, and I think that is our gift to the world.

CHAPTER THREE

VALUES AND PARADIGMS / CHOICES

THE ONLY WAY TO CLAIM YOUR VALUES IS TO KNOW THEM, AND TO LIVE THEM

"Claiming your values can mean leaving certain people behind.
This may be painful, but it may also be necessary."

—MARIAH EDGINGTON

VALUES

Values are who we are and what we do when no one's looking. We value honesty, integrity, gratitude, kindness, compassion, and respect. The Golden Rule is a cliché, but it's timeless. If you don't value yourself, you diminish the treatment you might expect from others.

Self-worth is a value that you can address with intention. No one grows plants with poison, so always make your thoughts and responses positive. Victor Frankl said, "Between stimulus and response there is a space. In that space is our power to choose our response. In our response lies our growth and our freedom." Mr. Frankl spent years in a Nazi concentration camp. His salvation derived from clinging to his values.

IGNORE THE NEGATIVE AND ASSUME THE POSITIVE

Everyone is fighting a battle we know nothing about. Assume the best of others, and they'll return the favor. Learn to avoid letting others "get under your skin," or "pull your chain." Better yet, explore the neurological aspect of interacting with others. This isn't as difficult or challenging as you imagine. Babies do this all the time. If you've ever been in a hospital nursery, you know that when one infant starts crying, very soon all the infants start crying. Why is this? Do they all soil their diapers at the same time? No. Do they all get hungry at once? No, they don't. It's simply because our brains are hardwired, even at a young age, to respond neurologically to the energy emanated by others. This has important applications for you as you claim your values. Here's an exercise you can use that's revealing and fun.

The next time you go to the grocery, smile at people as you pass them in the aisle. They'll pick up on the energy you're transmitting and smile back. This works in the opposite way as well. Frown and act angry, and others will reflect that negative emotion. If you arrive home happy and cheerful after an amazing day, and your spouse is upset, or mad, or depressed about the bills or their career, very soon you'll feel their pain, and your own mood and energy level will drop.

If you think about this concept, it means we have a powerful ability that we can use in good ways and in bad. We can quite literally change the way other people think, the way their brain functions, just by emitting certain signals to them and watching their responses. Savvy marketers know all about this. Indeed, there's a segment of the advertising business called "neuromarketing" that sniffs out better ways to manipulate us into purchasing products, trying markets, visiting restaurants, and ordering things online, all based on changing our neuro responses in ad copy.

So, the next time you face a particularly difficult meeting or encounter, or need to confront someone about their behavior, and you wish to stay true to your values, role play with yourself or a close friend using positive, encouraging thoughts and gestures. Be prepared that it may not go well and practice scripting to address that. The *Journey Well* guidebook contains examples of verbiage and messaging that helps you turn negative, disparaging messages into better, more positive ones. It also has an exercise for you to list your values in order to arrive at core values, those which are nonnegotiable.

Claiming your values can mean leaving certain people behind. This may be painful, but it may also be necessary. The signals you send out and those you receive enter your consciousness, too, after all.

"Stay in your lane!"

—MARIAH & BYRON

We once drove to Key West on Highway 1, the two-lane road that connects the Florida Keys. Every few miles we'd see a sign that read *Stay in Your Lane.* We adopted the phrase and use it whenever we veer outside conventions of courtesy. It's a bit like ACK, Always Choose Kind, a signal we use as an opportunity for kindness. "Stay in your lane" is a reminder to honor your values.

Everything is a choice. Make the choice to integrate your values into your daily life and take pride in the new you that emerges. Become the class act you want to spend time with.

PARADIGMS
(from Greek: *Paradeigma,* to show side by side)

"You are indeed paying for the label. Your label."

—BYRON EDGINGTON

Paradigms are the habits, behaviors, and restricting mechanisms that keep you *staying in your lane.* They're the social, economic, and behavioral guardrails stopping you if you reach *above your station.*

They determine the way you interact with others, what you eat, what topics you focus on, the TV shows you watch, the way you vote, and how you dress. They dictate your treatment of those outside your tribe, and your reaction to situations bad and good. Paradigms are also the script your inner critic recites from.

THEY DIRECT YOUR SAILS THE WAY YOUR FAVORABLE WIND BLOWS

There are people who won't go to the mailbox without makeup. Others go to Walmart in their PJs. These are paradigms in action. You're not even aware that these powerful forces exist, but they direct your sails whichever way your favorable wind blows, steering you toward familiar waters. It's hard work changing them, but you can choose to do so. It begins with taking the first step, deciding to choose the life you want.

Paradigms function in both directions. People living in thirty-room mansions would be uncomfortable in a trailer home. Those living in trailer homes would be uncomfortable in a thirty-room mansion.

If you need a new dress or new shoes, do you go to Target? If you enter a Nordstrom, do you look for the sale rack? That's your paradigm screaming *Caution! Expensive!* It's the obnoxious roommate in your attic yelling, *"you're paying for the label!"*

You are indeed paying for the label. Your label. Sadly, your paradigm is saying you're not good enough, that you don't deserve clothes from Nordstrom. You only deserve shoes from Payless, or shirts from Walmart. That's paying for a label too. Byron knows all about this from his time growing up second of ten.

Hand-me-downs were a reality in our house. First one up was the best one dressed. Mom bought dry milk powder, then she mixed it with water and poured it on our store-brand cornflakes. My folks would never have shopped at Nordstrom, sale rack or not. Our paradigms had "poor people" written all over them.

So how do you break free of stifling paradigms? How do you expose their actions in your life, cast them aside, and uncover the real you hiding under their "protective" blanket? The first step is to recognize them and how they affect you. Here's a short selection of common paradigms. Ask yourself how many apply to you:

"I'm not good at math, I could never do that problem."

"I can't afford a Gucci handbag."

"They hired me because they didn't have anyone else."

"I just got lucky, or I wouldn't be getting this award."

"Only rich people live there. I could never afford to."

"If I wear that, they'll think I'm showing off."

"My parents attend that church, so I have to."

"Everyone spends the holidays with family, so I have to be there."

"If I don't go to the (party/family function/religious rite) they'll say I'm being selfish."

Paradigms also reveal the limiting condition known as imposter syndrome. This mentality is prevalent in all age groups, genders, occupations, and levels of achievement. Albert Einstein suffered from imposter syndrome. He once remarked that he felt he was "an involuntary swindler." If Einstein battled a harsh inner critic you're in very good company.

PARADIGMS EAT INNOVATION FOR LUNCH

Here's something else Einstein said. "Everybody is a genius. But if you judge a fish by its ability to climb a tree, it will live its whole life believing that it is stupid." Notice the first segment of that quote: "Everybody is a genius." Think about what you do well. It's likely you worked hard to get where you are. Could someone else start today and do as well? Not likely.

Mariah understands the genius quotation, because impostor syndrome has held her back more than once during her long career as a nurse. To resist it, she recalled her ability to start IV lines on the tiniest newborns whose veins are all but invisible. But asking her to solve calculus problems or determine right from left in a split second is demanding that she climb a tree, fins and all. In my case, ask me to explain cryptocurrency, and I'm the trout in the tree as well. But ask me how to fly a helicopter and I'm all over it.

Impostor syndrome is limiting nonsense. If you're faced with its negative messaging, remember your superior skills, and the success you've had. If you shop for junk, you'll bring home junk. Shop for the good stuff, and you'll bring home the good stuff.

When you hear that critic calling you an impostor, use it as an opportunity to positively reinforce yourself with mindfulness, which is your best friend at times. Here's something that happened at our house recently, an example of how mindfulness can work in your favor. Mariah explains it.

I sensed that Byron was a bit out of sorts, a tad distant that morning. It's unlike either of us to feel estranged, as we simply treasure each other. Because of the intense feelings of love between us, we're highly attuned to the other's moods and behaviors. My mood was pretty dark. Finally, in response to something I said, Byron responded, "Well, I guess you'll just be angry with me all day."

His statement stopped me in my tracks. He was right; I *was* distressed and out of sorts. My emotional paradigms took over, guiding me in ways I never intended, and my beloved mate was taking the hit for it. I dug into what was bugging me, and we worked it out together. It was such an amazing lesson that I knew I had to share it.

We had been working on "forgiveness" in this book. My distress came from paradigms I learned at catechism lessons. At the tender age of seven, catholic kids make their "first confession," a rite meant to cleanse their souls of sin. When I entered the confessional at seven, I told the priest I *had* no sins. My statement elicited a blistering rebuke from the man behind the screen. He demanded that I manufacture a few sins so he could be benevolent and forgive me. When I wouldn't do it, he called my mother to come pick me up. Mom was not amused at my statement to the priest that I had no sins to confess.

Lest you wonder, dear reader, I've since rectified the situation; I now have many things which need *confessing*. These days, I bypass the priestly intervention and go straight to the source. It seems to work out better for all concerned.

The biggest takeaway is how important it is to be open to the process of growing through this journey. Opportunities will arise for you to question your old, worn-out paradigms. Take advantage of them. Review all the old ones. Don't be afraid to open yourself to the new ones. Though it may be painful, growth does cause discomfort, but the end result is worth the growing pains. This can be an exciting time for you. It can energize you and bring a new awareness as well.

As you become more aware of your limiting habits, you'll realize how much paradigms have to do with your inner critic. As it turns out, none of it is productive. The guardrails of your mind interrupt you when you need to claim your power. At that moment, the rascal demands that you confess your sins and stop making a fool of yourself. The only way to defeat it is to listen to your inner cheerleader instead.

Regardless of how much experience you have, how old you are, or what the sign on your office door says, you have a label. That labeling might match the paradigm you've battled all your life. Choose to change that image, and you'll emerge as a new and amazing you!

ONE OF THE MOST POWERFUL VOICES YOU'LL EVER HEAR IS YOUR OWN, SAYING YOUR NAME

In the guidebook, and on our website, we offer the "I AM" exercise. It's a simple acknowledgment that reciting positive, affirming words to yourself builds you up and silences your inner critic.

Here's the short version of it: whatever follows I AM follows you.

> I AM...Beautiful
> I AM...Competent
> I AM...Worthy

The "I AM" exercise orients your mind toward positive messages about yourself. It raises your energy, and it raises you. Use this exercise several times a day, and soon you'll believe it. I AM...Determined to claim my place as a wonderful person.

Mirror work is also a powerful way to remove self-doubt, shame, guilt, or feelings of inability. Do mirror work for a time, and you'll be amazed at the results. It will seem awkward at first, but after a while it becomes second nature, and the warmth and positive feeling it brings will energize you.

Stand in front of a mirror. Look at yourself and say "I love you—", followed by your name. This practice will seem awkward at first. Keep doing it. In a week or maybe two you'll sense a major change in your self-esteem. Remember, what you focus on expands. Do mirror work every day as you go through your routine morning ritual, brushing your teeth, applying makeup, shaving, or just because you need the affirmation.

Mirror work helps you discard old, tired paradigms. But it also helps you put blame for your past missteps behind you. One of the most powerful voices you'll ever hear is your own saying your name, followed by *I forgive you* and *I love you*. Before a meeting, say, *I see why they hired you!* If you're about to interview for a new position, face a mirror and say, *The job is yours, congratulations!* There's no better way to silence the inner critic than to recognize and claim your power.

If you blame yourself for past missteps, your success will be elusive, and your journey rough and uncertain. You'll have a hard time taking off and soaring to the heights we want to take you. Remember, there's a reason they call it the past. Moving forward, every second that goes by creates a new past. So move forward and leave it behind. It can't be changed anyway, so looking back is wasted energy.

Imagine the wonderful things you've done in your life. Consider the successes you've had, the people you've helped, the challenges you've overcome, and the people who look up to you. You relied on your values to accomplish those things. Imagine your younger self, the child who passed all their classes, who won entry to college, landed a career. Think about the gentle and loving person who made someone's life easier. That's you. Think of an old, tired family, religious, social, or other paradigm that didn't serve you well so you created a new one. That's you, too.

You're a beautiful person who's determined to journey well. Those are *your* successes. Be proud of them. Don't allow past missteps to take you backward. Instead, take off straight ahead, keep moving forward into a fresh, new wind, explore your own success, and journey well.

**HERE ARE THREE IMPORTANT POINTS ABOUT VALUES
AND PARADIGMS AND IMPOSTOR SYNDROME:**

★ Assume the best of others, and they'll return the favor.

★ Live in congruence with your values.

★ Paradigms are also the script your inner critic recites from.

ACTION STEPS:

- Think of a paradigm you carry with you. Now imagine moving away from it, embracing a new concept, a new perspective.

- Listen to your inner critic. When you hear it, celebrate that you noticed it squawking, and took action.

- Give yourself an affirmation. I AM—<u>More</u> than enough!

- Check the *Journey Well* guidebook for more affirmations.

PERSONAL JOURNEY

CORY WARFIELD

"I CREATE LINKEDIN INFLUENCERS |Tech founder Advisor | Promoter | Growth Coach | Connector | Amplifier | Strategist."

~

As for my values, I don't know that I live them, I kind of embody them. They would be empathy and reciprocity. I try to view everything through those two lenses. I don't do things to get things back, but every time I put good out, I seem to get good back.

Once a quarter I give someone a scholarship for school that can't afford it, and just today one of them contacted me in tears. She started out with 90 followers, and now she has 2,400. Her posts are getting 100,000 views, thousands of likes, she has feelers out for 7 jobs and today one of them came through, from a guy I introduced her to. He's going to be paying her $250.00 a week, so a thousand American dollars a month. She's Nigerian, so that's a lot of money to her. Her husband lost his job, and they have kids, and she was absolutely elated.

I got a message on WhatsApp, saying, "Cory hiring her is going to be a life changer for me." You try to do everything in good faith, and it comes back ten-fold, a million-fold, whatever it might be.

As for the time I was living on the street, I'd have money for a couple slices of pizza, and I'd give one away, and empathy and non-judgment came out of that. I was a waiter for 20 years, and I started having the 'servant in the castle' mentality, and I think that's where the non-judgment idea came from as well.

I heard about this website built by the Israelis called Shareit*. They offer a platform to sell things, and they were arranging for Israelis and Palestinians to put books on others' doorsteps, and I thought this could promote world peace. And I met with the chairman of that company, and he asked if I knew anyone in Brazil, and I said, okay, you're kidding me, right? I live down there! I fell in love with the place. It's one of those things that's cool and funny at the same time, so I couldn't say no to him.

I knew I was smart, and I believed in myself. What influenced my path the most, I think, was the desire to always be improving. My grandfather had a lot of money, but I never saw him work a day in his life, so I learned you can work smarter not harder. I know I can go out today and make six figures, then give it away, and make more tomorrow. I don't stockpile. I'm not a gambler. I love to give it away. Philanthropy is a beautiful thing.

*https://www.ushareit.com

CHAPTER FOUR

WORDS ARE IMPORTANT / POSITIVITY

YOUR WORDS CRAFT
YOUR WORLD

"What we say and what we hear are
critically important to what we believe."
—BYRON EDGINGTON

These letters: **abcdefghijklmnopqstwxyz** form every word in the English language. They can be put together to build us up or bring us down. Just glancing at them, you might not see or discern the power of their composition, their ability to suppress or impress, to diminish or elevate, to praise or damn. But those twenty-six letters can be used in any manner we choose. They may seem small and unimpressive, but they craft our world, our dreams, and our lives.

What words are taking up valuable real estate inside your mind? Many people internalize negative words, the cannots and should nots and don't evers. You may have heard words of limitation and withholding, but seldom words of capacity, ability, and access. Few people hear words describing a world without limits. Here's our message: Your world is limitless. That nine-letter word defines all we're describing in *Journey Well.*

You may have received kind, well-intended words along the way. But due to your fear response, or your harsh inner critic, your mind absorbed hurtful judgments instead of praise. Our brains didn't evolve to think. They evolved to keep us alive and safe. It's the negative, hurtful messages that burrow deep into your mind, and stick with tenacity becoming louder over time. They have the unbelievable ability to become believable, and to become your reality.

If you grew up hearing no, never, not, and don't, words of hesitation and fear that habitually pulled you lower, you were always poised to fail. Words that picked relentlessly at your self-esteem eventually replaced the empowered feeling with a sense of lack. If you grew up hearing words without limit, you know you can fly.

WORDS CRAFT YOUR LIFE

The *obnoxious roommate in your attic* can linger all your life unless you actively dispel it with positive, affirming words.

What we say and what we hear are critically important to what we believe. Neuroscience confirms this. Many studies have proven that our word choice has a great influence on our self-esteem and the way we perceive others. In one of these studies, people in a shopping mall were asked to write words associated with old age, senility, and decline. The next group was asked to write words about youth, energy, and opportunity. The first group walked away slowly, shoulders sagging, frowns on their faces. The second group of people skipped away, filled with energy and smiling.

This is simply how our minds work. They absorb whatever thoughts and feelings we feed them. Depending on their status, either positive or negative, words have a powerful impact on who you are and how you see yourself.

We process words and phrases in a way that either encourages us or makes us hesitant. Here's an example. *This steak is 25 percent fat,* vs *this steak is 75 percent lean.* Guess which phrase sells more steak? That's right, the one with 75 percent in it. Same amount of fat vs lean, but the words conveying fat content are different.

Neuroscience has also found that our word choices with other people create a negative or positive response in *their* brains. When we say thank you, the standard response is *you're welcome.* But saying *my pleasure,* or *delighted to help you,* causes a much stronger positive reaction in the listener's brain.

The words you're reading right now are altering your thoughts and your life with every syllable and every meaning. Words bring you pleasure, emotion, ideas, opportunities, and a sense of acclaim when you succeed at something.

Yes! Of course! Naturally! Always! Good for you! Fantastic! Positive, affirming words and phrases like these add energy to your mind and raise you up. As you just read those words and phrases, you envisioned their meaning, and your energy level rose. *No way! Forget it! Get out of here! Never! Not now!* What happened to your energy level? It dropped, didn't it. Words matter.

Imagine the most inspiring words ever spoken: "I have a dream," and "Ask what you can do for your country," and "Yes we can!" The speakers understood their power, and the effect they had on listeners' minds. Those words changed lives and changed worlds. When we don't take full advantage of the power of stringing letters together into positive words, we miss the powerful message they convey.

Read this string of letters aloud. Say them slowly, one by one.

ABCDEFGHIJKLMNOPQSTWXYZ

What stands out? What stopped you?

What's missing?

Are you fully present and positive for yourself every day? R-U?

It isn't possible to avoid all negative chatter, especially these days when social media are filled with dark, regressive words. You need to reframe negative thoughts and turn them around, finding a positive instead. Here are some suggestions: Instead of *those people always...* Flip that around to *isn't it amazing...* Instead of *what an awful thing...* Try *look at the opportunity!* When you're in a career setting, you might hear the inner critic challenging your perceived lack of competence. Instead of saying *I'm not qualified for this,* or *they're going to find out I can't...* try, *they see my potential,* or *everything I've done has led me to this point.* Stand in your competence. You are <u>More</u> than enough.

POURING HAPPINESS INTO PEOPLE'S CUPS

A recent YouTube video featured a barista at an airport coffee shop. Her attitude was exemplary, and her words were priceless. It was during the holidays, and she was at work, mixing talls and lattes, meeting travelers' needs. When asked why she was so cheerful *just pouring coffee,* she said, "I'm not pouring coffee; I'm pouring happiness into people's cups." See the difference?

Here are a few reasons to use positive, uplifting words to be fulfilled and happy yourself. Other people who hear you using those positive words will hear you accenting the positive, and one of two things will happen: They'll emulate you and be grateful for your refreshing attitude. Or they'll dismiss you as naïve and out of touch with reality. Guess which group we're in?

What other people think of you is none of your business. Which tribe do you prefer? The happy, positive, grateful tribe of people who feel good about themselves? The tribe that understands how fulfilling it is to pour happiness into people's cups? That's the tribe we choose.

Here's another reason to use positive, uplifting words. When you use them, other people stand taller because of it, and so do you. Using kind, supportive words is the pebble splashing into the smooth, clear water of the pond, rippling out in directions you can never predict. As the fellow sipped his cup of happiness, it filled him with more than warmth and caffeine.

Use kind words every day, and you'll gain a reputation for dispensing kindness to everyone, for *pouring happiness in people's cups*. Someday your words will arrive as a gift to someone who needs them at that moment, and just the way they're wrapped. It's a great reputation to have.

People are listening to what you preach to see if it's what you practice, if your words match what you do. The technical word for this is praxis. Praxis is from Greek, and it's where the English word practice comes from. It's the actions we take, the congruence we *practice*, and it begins with our words. Especially now with so much distance between some people's words and their actions, praxis is critical to your message and to ours.

Words are the medium we use to either lift ourselves up in a positive growth mindset, or to maintain a fixed position on our old, rutted ground in a negative mindset. How important, then, that the words you use with yourself are positive, affirming, and elevating. Always choosing words that build yourself and others up is the key to creating a successful life. When people hear words of limitless possibility coming from you, they'll realize they can become the amazing person they have a right to be as well.

THOSE WHO MATTER MOST TO YOU ARE THOSE WHO MATTER MOST

If you're unsure how your words might be received, or if you hesitate to use them, remember that the people who are *supposed* to get your message *will* get it. Those who matter most to you are those who matter most.

Here's another coffee shop tale with a barista on the other end of the energy spectrum. She was the one needing help. Mariah tells the story:

I was in line at a local Starbucks outlet at 8 am. Behind the counter, the young barista worked frantically, preparing products, taking orders and payments, doing everything required because she was the only employee there that morning.

One after another, the young woman fixed lattes, talls, grandes, ventis, and assorted confections. She processed payments, cleaned equipment, and greeted people all by herself, with a line of customers waiting at one of the busiest times of the day. It was clear that she took her job seriously, but also clear that she was frazzled trying to keep up, and already tired at 8 am.

A fellow ahead of me in line looked at the girl, and with absolutely no judgment intended, he merely said, "It looks like you could use some help."

The girl shook her head and said nothing.

I got her attention and said, "I just want you to know that you're doing an incredible job. Thank you so much!"

The girl's face blossomed in a smile. "Thank *you* so much for saying that," she said. "You have no idea what it meant to me."

This admonition goes for you as well. Don't hesitate to reach out to yourself. Look in the mirror again, and salute yourself for a job well done, for even the smallest success. Make it a habit of catching yourself succeeding, call yourself out on it, and take the reward with a smile. Words matter, especially when they come from a source of authority, in other *words*, from you!

Both scenarios from Starbucks present a way you can use words to make the world better. Fully embrace the impulse to love others and to tell them that you love them. Affirm them out loud and assume they're part of the "family" you've built around yourself. Tell them you're grateful for them and the gift they bring. They may not respond at first. But they might respond in a way you never expected. The person you meet may be the holiday barista pouring happiness when people need it most. Or they may be the young, frazzled barista who says *you have no idea what your words meant to me.* Either way, their positive response will give you back a warm glow that lasts long after you finish your grande latte.

Here's an exercise we love that reinforces the power of words. We mentioned this before, but it's very important, so here it is again. Remember, whatever follows I AM follows *you.* After each I AM, add a positive word or phrase, and you'll feel the energy level rise. Try it:

I AM...Amazing.

I AM...Intelligent.

I AM...Creative.

I AM...Beautiful.

I AM..._____.

I AM..._____.

You'll find this exercise again in the guidebook and on our website with several other resources.

In *The Summer Day*, Poet Mary Oliver wrote, *Tell me what is it you plan to do with your one wild and precious life?* This is *your* one wild and precious life we're talking about. There are people who need you and who look up to you. Leading your precious life lifts *you* up. But it also lifts them. This is your gift and your obligation. The I AM exercise is a powerful practice. Whatever follows I AM, follows you.

You've heard that *done* is better than perfect, yet how many people fear the phrase "not good enough" rattling around in their brains? Allowing only positive words to enter is the key. As Dr. Wayne Dyer advised, "Don't let the elusive present moment get used up by thoughts that aren't in the here and now."

Are you letting negative words aimed at yourself grab your attention? If so, become your own gatekeeper and flip the negatives into positives. Remember, as Louise Hay often wrote, the point of power is now. The world is harsh enough without piling negativity onto yourself. Allow a ray of positivity to shine into your own soul.

Know your core values, live your core values, and those positive, elevating words will flow without effort. Live a life worth emulating by speaking your positive, affirming truth, and you'll be a leader who lights the world. You're an amazing human, a class act. Be proud of all you're bringing to the world, especially your words. Words matter.

WORDS CAN BE MOST IMPORTANT WHEN THEY'RE NOT SAID

Here's an addendum. Sometimes words left unspoken are more powerful than the loudest proclamation. Sometimes people notice you far more for staying silent when others are preaching. Cherish those moments of silence and seek them out. Blaise Pascal said, "All the world's problems can be traced to our inability to sit silently in a room alone." Remaining silent is a lost art, and a difficult practice, but well worth the effort. Words can be most important and most powerful when they're not said.

The universe speaks in silence. Musicians say the beauty of a composition is found in the space between the notes. Listen to the most beautiful music ever written, the ninth symphony of Antonin Dvořák from the New World, *anything* written by Mozart, Samuel Barber's adagio for strings, the Beethoven Violin Concerto in D, or your favorite piece of music, and you'll hear the pure, soul-stirring silence between each sublime note.

The only imperative you have in this life is to realize your own magnificence. Imperative is the right word. To live the life you dream of—the full, rich, positive life that's a guide for others—you must use words that craft that life, full, rich, positive words. Here are two words we use to create the beautiful, fulfilling life we chose: *Journey Well.*

HERE ARE THREE IMPORTANT POINTS FROM THIS CHAPTER:

★ What negative words take up valuable real estate inside your mind?

★ Your world is <u>limitless.</u> That nine-letter word defines all we're describing in *Journey Well.*

★ The obnoxious roommate in your attic can linger all your life unless you actively dispel it with positive, affirming words.

ACTION STEPS:

✎ Next time you visit a coffee shop, a grocery checkout, a fast-food store, look for a way to compliment a worker.

✎ Today, leave someone with "the impression of increase."

✎ Give someone who needs it encouragement and acknowledge their hard work. They'll feel better, and so will you.

✎ Use nouns instead of verbs: Not I write every day, but I AM a writer. Instead of I run five miles a day, I AM a runner. Not I will get out of debt, but I AM prosperous. (The last one erases negativity as well.)

PERSONAL JOURNEY
RACHEL BECK

Rachel Beck shares her thoughts on the importance of words, and how they create the life and world we want. As a minority American, she's heard and witnessed how words can be used to harm and to heal. Rachel Beck is the author of *Finding Your Way When Life Changes Your Plans: A Memoir of Adoption, Loss of motherhood and Remembering Home.*

～

Words are everything. Everything you say, your writing, your speaking has consequences. We all have a filter from our brain to our mouth, whether we choose to use it or not. Everything we say impacts another human being's life. I'm not one of those people who say 'hurt people', that's not a category I fall into. I think we're responsible for the things we say, what we write, what we do, even our body language.

I've been a victim of bullying, the victim of being called some of the worst names in the world, so I choose not to treat people that way. I've been on the other side of it from complete strangers.

We can do a switch every day. How do we want to be remembered? I don't want people to say "she hurt my feelings." Now, of course people do that, but they'll say she didn't go out of her way to do it.

I'm not one of those people who believes everything is forgivable. I think once the damage is done, you've said something so horrible, you could say you're sorry, but you could have prevented it in the first place with the words you choose.

When I hear _I can't_ I think _I can._ There are people still telling me that. When I hear _I shouldn't,_ I think _I should._ I played sports all my life, and some of my best lessons came from my coaches, telling me _I should,_ and so forth.

When I hear, _I hate it when..._ a lot comes into my mind: racism, unnecessary hate. I hate that some people want to dominate others. There's no reason for that, ever. I don't think anyone should ever be a victim. I hate it that I've heard _I should leave this country,_ when members of my own family have served this country. I hate it as a minority American woman that when I get up every day I have to give 200%, when others have to give only 100% because some have already made an assumption about me.

When I hear code words, like people want to say (The) N word or mention a dog. If it's about Jewish people, there are comments about money. It's not just code words; it's body language, like a tilt of the head, and words as well, like _Oh, honey, are you sure you can afford to shop here?_ Or the vague comment about _your kind._ Or they might say _'would you mind waiting in the front of the restaurant?'_ versus coming inside.

My reaction is for safety first, then I'll spend my money somewhere else! There's a look, you know? There's a look they use.

I created my show because I'm looking for leaders. I look for them every day, people who need to be out in the world. I was told that if the ladder was given to you, you need to pass it down to the next kind soul. That's what we need to blanket the world with. The other side is organized. We need to organize all the kind people.

CHAPTER FIVE

BOUNDARIES / DIGNITY

BOUNDARIES
=
DIGNITY

"Boundaries are evidence of strength, since many people
fail to use them, while suffering in silence."
—MARIAH EDGINGTON

A major step in claiming your new life and your new self is to establish boundaries. Personal boundaries are more important than ever, and now is an excellent time to claim yours, especially those you wish to establish between yourself and people who tend to be demanding, negative, abusive, rude, or manipulative.

First, let us reiterate that you are a worthy person, that you deserve your position and the boundaries you claim. We've said it before, but here it is again: You are <u>More</u> than enough. You have no obligation to go beyond what you're comfortable with or willing to do. You are your own unique and vital self and anyone who won't acknowledge that, or who violates your boundaries, must understand that their behavior is simply unacceptable.

Your boundaries are who you are. They're what you believe and the way you perceive your world. You need those boundaries as much as the air you breathe. If someone says you have no right to feel that way, ask if you have a right to feel hot or to feel hungry?

You need boundaries around such issues as kids, family, modern intrusions like social media and TV, and around those with other religious persuasions, or even our own at times. You must create boundaries to shield you from so-called crepe hangers who traffic in morbid and depressing news. Your work environment is an area where boundaries are especially important, since you spend a lot of time there and can't readily escape the intrusions.

Areas of life you may not have considered creating boundaries for are such places as loud and distracting restaurants, the tyranny of movie theaters, concert halls, and other venues you can't graciously leave without feeling embarrassed or singled out. You need boundaries against such things as phone solicitations or hard-sell marketers. Some people might consider these boundaries evidence of weakness or timidity. They're evidence of strength since many people use them while suffering in silence.

Parents can be the most intrusive people we encounter. Especially if you have children, your parents may intrude on your life and those of your children more than they did when you were little. The boundaries you need in this case can be difficult to build and maintain, but they're also necessary. Start early by outlining exactly what position and interventions you'd like your parents to take with the grandkids, and what your expectations are of them. Remember, there's a fundamental difference between responsible to and responsible for. As an adult, you're no longer responsible to your parents. You're responsible for your children.

Learn a lesson from your children. Babies are very good at announcing their boundaries. A toddler has no hesitation to scream when his toy is taken away, or when she's forced into a bath, or to eat her corn instead of her cake. Children don't have societal pressure to conform or to stay silent about their needs and desires. They yell right away, letting us know when they're upset, tired, cranky, or dissatisfied. You can learn a lot about boundaries from a hungry, cranky two-year-old with a dirty diaper.

TELLING SOMEONE TO *JUST CALM DOWN*
HAS NEVER CAUSED THEM TO *CALM DOWN*

The demand to conform starts when you're young. It's usually very subtle, such as when a grownup tells you to "be nice and give your uncle a hug" or "kiss your grandma or she'll be sad". But you didn't want to hug your uncle or kiss your grandmother, you were forced to do so. When you refused, you were labeled touchy or hard to get along with.

As adults, your boundaries were eroded or ignored by social pressure to be nice, causing you to act, speak, and perform in order to blend in, to kiss or hug that relative you never liked. Speaking up for yourself, declining an invitation, refusing food, drink, or dessert, or saying no to a physical intrusion makes you uncomfortable. But you have a right to your feelings. Do you have a right to be thirsty, or a right to be thirty-seven years old? It's a nonsense question. Telling someone to *just calm down* has never caused them to *calm down*. Feelings are real, and they're the best indicator of your need for boundaries.

If you give in to pressure, and then feel ashamed or violated and angry, that's your inner voice saying your boundaries have been crossed. When you establish clear boundaries, friends recognize them, and those who honor them become people you can trust. It's those who ignore your boundaries that you need to be wary of. If you alienate them, so be it. A good friend is often better than an old friend.

On the other hand, assuming people *can't do without you*, or will be sad/hurt/angry/confused by your refusal to do what they want, is assuming they're unable to do for themselves. It's your way of saying they need you, that their boundaries are porous and ill-defined as well. Boundaries work both ways. The people who sense your new boundaries may very well see their own need for them, and that would be a good thing.

So, what's the best way to establish boundaries? First, be aware of your feelings of apprehension, dis-ease, or even anger. Those reactions are there, and they're real. Don't let anyone tell you your feelings are wrong or inappropriate. There can be nothing *wrong* with feelings. They tell you what's happening in real time.

Next, you can start an *I have a right to...* list. I have a right to refuse going somewhere, accepting an invitation, to do whatever it is that stirs your anger and discomfort. Start with a short list, three or four items, and before long you may see that you do need boundaries after all.

Have you ever been called selfish? It just means you put your needs ahead of others'. There's not a thing wrong with that. On the airplane, you're told to put on your own mask first, then your child's. That boundary is for your good and for the child's as well. Assuming someone else can't do something without your help can set up an unhealthy codependency. When you think about it, the assumption is arrogant and hurtful to that person. It makes them appear helpless.

Here's an antidote to the impulse to dive in unasked and help someone. Put your hand in a bucket of water. When you pull it out, the hole that remains is how much your help is truly needed. In other words, they'll get along fine without you. Your ego may tell you otherwise, but then our egos cause lots of trouble in many situations.

Another way to establish clear boundaries is to say no. If you're asked to do something, or go along when you don't want to, just say no. No may be the most difficult word there is to say, and to mean, but as writer Anne LaMott said, "no" is a complete sentence. And when you say "no," that makes your "yes" stronger when something else comes up.

Another way to create your boundaries is making an "*I don't have to...*" list. "I don't have to..."

- ...answer the phone on the first ring, or ever.
- ...respond to a text.
- ...add to a Facebook thread right away (or ever).
- ...go with friends to that bar/restaurant/concert/movie.
- ...drink that/smoke that/get high on that.
- ...ignore how she/he talks about me.
- ...lend her/him that money, assuming it's gone forever.
- ...go to parents,' siblings,' in-laws' events.

You'll make your own "I don't have to..." list, but this is a good start.

Here's another way: Tell friends and family you're creating boundaries for yourself and make an "*I'm going to...*" week, month, year, or forever list. Here's an example. "I'm going to..."

- ...be there for (a birthday/anniversary/thanksgiving/holiday) period, this week/month/year/ever if I decide to.
- ...choose my response to the sister/brother/mother/father who doesn't honor my boundaries.
- ...stop eating (fill in the blank) because I don't like it.
- ...find a job I love.

≋ ...help her/him out of debt because I choose to.

The list can include items you've brooded about for a long time, the ways you've felt used and abused by certain people. Instead of an "I choose not to..." list, find a positive action instead.

Don't be surprised when you get negative feedback anyway. Remember, you don't have to explain your boundaries. When friends or family invite you out and you don't wish to go, or they ask for help with a project and you don't want to help, say I choose not to and leave it at that. They may ask why. You don't owe them an explanation.

This isn't easy. Our impulse is always to explain and say I don't have time, or I have another commitment. But you don't owe anyone that. Yes, the risk is that they won't like you, or they'll say you're being difficult. The important thing is for *you* to like you.

You may have heard the term "gaslighting." It's used to dismiss our feelings of suspicion. Gaslighting is an old strategy that devious, insecure people use to convince you your feelings are invalid. They'll swear you're mistaken, or that you're crazy to question them about something when you know very well what you saw or heard is true. You did see your companion steal the tip money from the table or slip a thumb drive into their purse at Best Buy. You did hear them tell their mother they're in the library when they were perched on a barstool next to you. The gaslighter claims it never happened. You made it up or misconstrued it. "That's not what I meant" is a common trope among gaslighters.

Mariah was once asked by a nurse colleague to cover up the woman's illicit use of patient narcotics. This person implicated them both to save their job, trying to make Mariah clean up her mess. It didn't work, but it was extremely uncomfortable for a time. As difficult as it might be, don't back down. Trust your instincts and your truth. If your gut tells you something's wrong, then something is wrong.

Mariah used her well-honed instincts many times in her career to help her patients when they needed help. Despite pushback from colleagues at times, including from physicians on occasion, she knew when a patient was in trouble, and she insisted that they receive treatment. In my aviation career, my intuition told me many times that my gut was on to something. Several times I sensed something amiss, took it seriously, and escaped an incident. This strength came from honoring boundaries.

What is it you fear, and why do you need boundaries? The fear is often of being rejected if you don't conform. It's fear of being labeled high maintenance or selfish or odd. It's the fear that others won't understand you and to be understood is one of our basic needs as humans.

This isn't just about physical boundaries, either. This is about emotional and psychological boundaries as well, the intrusive nature of seemingly innocent, everyday actions that disregard your emotional space. This is about your right and responsibility to yourself to create and observe distance from others that shows them—and you—that your agency is to be honored and respected.

This is also about so-called intellectual boundaries, the right to maintain your values and integrity in an increasingly transparent world.

YOU ALWAYS HAVE A RIGHT TO DECLARE YOUR BOUNDARIES, WITH NO EXPLANATION TO ANYONE BUT YOURSELF

The message is that family history and the first relationships you ever had made it both difficult and imperative that you establish boundaries. Women are not automatically given their agency in this society. It's something you must demand for yourself, and society always fights back, it seems.

The loving conflict between fathers and sons, between mothers and daughters is an entrenched narrative for which no resolution exists. As parents ourselves, we understand that the best gift we can give our children is the ability to establish boundaries, not just between friends and colleagues, but between them and us as well.

For women readers, a man may have assumed authority over you, despite their lack of moral authority. You may have siblings who received preference in various ways, especially if they're male. You may have challenges with your mother like those you have with other women. Mothers tend to dismiss their daughters' aspirations if they don't match traditional expectations. Boundaries are needed to establish your own identity, and to differentiate yourself, especially in a large family. You know very well who you are, and who you are not. Don't be afraid to say it aloud and own it.

SOME PEOPLE ARE LIKE THE OLD TOWN CRIER IN REVERSE, WARNING THAT ALL IS NOT WELL! WITH THEIR MORBID ATTITUDE AND OMINOUS WARNINGS, THEY CAN TRANSGRESS OUR BOUNDARIES TOO

Boundaries do more than differentiate you. They create a safe space that allows you to see your world in a different way. They let you see the endless possibilities constraints keep hidden. Because of our recent study of the better, more affirming menu of positive, uplifting messaging, we've seen a change in our own behavior, attitude, opportunities, and fortunes. That fortune isn't in money; it's in the way we see and sense our abundant world. The change came about partly because we've established boundaries that allow in only positive, affirming thoughts and actions. Here's a deeper discussion of this. See if it resonates with you.

We know a person who is an inveterate crepe hanger. This person is immersed in the daily, even hourly tragic, scandalous, explosive bad news. Sharing mayhem and madness seems to be an obligation with this person. The old town crier in reverse, warning that all is not well! With their morbid attitude and ominous warnings, they can transgress our boundaries too. We had to establish strict boundaries around this behavior because it is, quite frankly, depressing and corrosive to good mental health.

The other aspect of this is the flood of such negative and chaotic news streaming into our living rooms, kitchens, and bedrooms these days. The boundary necessary against this wash of woe is simple: turn the TV off. Remember, whether to be a spectator to the electronic inundation we're subjected to today or not is a choice. If you swim in a dirty river, you'll get wet—and dirty.

When Mariah worked as a nurse, she'd often enter a patient's room to do whatever was needed, and many times the TV was on, the noise and intrusion making it difficult for her to do an assessment or a procedure. She'd simply ask the patient if they'd mind if she muted the television. Most patients appreciated her asking for permission and generally agreed to it. It was one of her boundaries while at work, helping her do the job efficiently and without compromise.

Work environments can be the most challenging and the most necessary places to establish boundaries. Especially for nurses, the opportunities for being bullied by patients, doctors, and colleagues is always present, even after many years and much experience. The need for boundaries can be met with opposition from those with borderline skills. It's not unusual for colleagues to revert to bullying to hide their own sense of incompetence. Oddly, the inner voice telling them they're not good enough can make them lash out at others whose skills are better.

Another boundary to consider is one you need against people assuming they know you, and that you share their values. You've no doubt answered your doorbell to find salespeople or evangelists of one creed or another anxious to share their wares with you. We respect others' beliefs, and their ambition to spread that belief in a system that works for them. But they can be quite persistent. Letting them know right away, with as much courtesy as you can muster, that you're simply not interested is a good boundary to build. Put yourself in their position. You don't want people wasting your time either.

ONCE YOU'RE CLEAR ABOUT THE BOUNDARY YOU'VE SET, IT'S MUCH EASIER TO SHARE IT WITH OTHERS AND TO SENSE WHEN IT'S ABOUT TO BE CROSSED

The mantra of all news outlets is *if it bleeds, it leads.* In other words, bad news catches viewers' eyeballs and helps the station reap advertising dollars. You never hear a reporter claim that *dozens of airplanes took off and landed safely today.* It's a sad comment on modern life that switching off resources that keep us informed may be necessary for our serenity and peace.

Another time to establish boundaries is while reconnecting with an estranged friend or child. If you've willed these people back into your life, and wish to reconnect with them, it may be the best thing you can do for yourself and for them to be clear what the boundaries are. You may need to state that certain topics are off limits. That certain people are to be left out, and certain dates, events, and interactions are not something you wish to revisit.

Boundaries are defined and established in several ways, some of which you may not have considered. First, determine what your boundaries are. Make a list of items that jump out at you. Put it aside and review it in a few days. Once you're clear about the boundary you've set, it's much easier to share it with others and to sense when it's about to be crossed.

- Use expressions that show people boundaries while being gentle and courteous.
- Remember, "<u>NO</u>" is a complete sentence.
- You could advise people of the new boundary and test it among loving friends.
- Write boundaries in whatever detail you feel is necessary.
- Speak up when those boundaries are crossed and make sure the transgressor understands. This isn't easy, of course, but nothing worthwhile ever is.

Here are a few expressions you can use:

- "No, thank you. That doesn't work for me. Why do you ask?"
- "That hurt my feelings. Please don't do that again."

Or learn to simply say no without explanation.
Remember, "NO" is complete sentence.

In the *Journey Well* guidebook, you'll find more techniques to create and enforce your boundaries.

Boundaries are needed today more than ever. Those boundaries will help keep you on the road toward the better you, the brighter life you envision as you make the choice to set and maintain them as you continue to *Journey Well.*

HERE ARE THREE IMPORTANT POINTS FOR YOU TO KEEP IN MIND WHEN ESTABLISHING PERSONAL, EMOTIONAL, OR PSYCHOLOGICAL BOUNDARIES:

★ You have no obligation to go beyond what you're comfortable with, or safe, or willing to do.

★ Discern the most intrusive people you'll encounter. Start early and write your boundaries. Be gentle, but firm.

★ Once you're clear about the particular boundary you've set, it's much easier to share it with others and to sense when it's about to be crossed.

ACTION STEPS:

≋ Make a list of recent times you said yes when you wanted to say no.

≋ At the next opportunity, say no thanks and go back to reading your book, especially if it's *Journey Well*.

≋ Role play how to say no without feeling guilt or shame, and without feeling like you owed an explanation.

≋ Role play with a friend and help each other build up those boundaries muscles.*

*See the *Journey Well* guidebook for more

PERSONAL JOURNEY

DIANE WYZGA

"Coaching Professional Women Who Are Ready to Confidently Convey
Their Story to Be Seen, Heard, Understood *&* Listened to |
Your Story Strategizer & Founder Engaged Storyism® Method."

This piece on boundaries is courtesy of Diane Wyzga, J.D. Ms
Wyzga is a survivor who understands boundaries better than most.
She long ago decided to let go of the handlebars and go along for
the ride.

Diane Wyzga posts her 60 seconds of wisdom from Whidbey
Island Washington: #StoriesFromWomenWhoWalk

Imagine this: In the space of 9 months, you lose your marriage, your mother, and your attorney position. How did I
get there? More importantly, how did I get out? In time, I'd
be able to fully appreciate what those 9 months birthed.

I was in my 30s before I married. An educated, independent professional woman. But I never learned this: You
don't get married because someone asks you to; you get
married because you want to. The man I married was a
well-liked president and CEO of a corporation. I had mis-
givings. I couldn't pin them down. A week before the wed-

ding, I told my mom who said what someone probably told her: "You've been independent for so long, you've just got cold feet."

I knew I would be Wife #3. Isn't Number 3 a lucky number? Not in my case. In time, I learned that my husband had a problem with impotence. Like many women I figured something was wrong with *me*. Isn't that often the case? We take on issues that don't belong to us, and we allow our boundaries to be not only crossed but trampled on.

Yet, I was willing to accept what I thought was security. We had a brother-sister relationship, took very good vacations, and worked hard in our professions. Time passed. Ten years of time. Looking back, it's like that old story of the frog sitting in a pot of water on a stove. The flame is turned on, the water heats up, but it's so gradual that the frog doesn't notice until she is well and truly cooked.

You know how they say that the wife is the last to know? It's not just a saying. In my case there was also denial. Until in late November of that year when he came home late with a shallow excuse, I knew I had to face what I was afraid of, poverty, shame, solitude to name a few things.

I asked a divorce lawyer friend what to do. Make sure you have access to all important papers and bank accounts, she told me. You don't want to be locked out. Going through the files in his desk drawer I came across a small yellow Post-it with the name Ash and a phone number. I called the number. Ash was the working name of a prostitute who, I would come to find out, had been with my husband for the better part of a year. When confronted, my husband gave denials and then excuses, "If you had only been more [fill in the blank] I wouldn't have been forced to do this."

Meanwhile, mom had developed shingles, but it was a precursor to lymphoma. From Thanksgiving to the following Easter mom's doctor misdiagnosed her condition until she was in Stage 4 lymphoma; mom would die 5 months later.

You know how things come in 3s? My law firm was engaged in a merger with a very large corporation. I wasn't part of the deal. In 9 months' time I had no marriage, no mother, no job. I fell into a deep hole.

What happened next? There was bare-bones alimony. I was a lost soul. An organic farm in town posted a Help Wanted sign. I offered my CV to the farmer who was looking for someone to work in the farm stand at $9 an hour. I took it. At the bank that held the interest-only mortgage on the house, the banker assured me she was going to do everything possible to get me a real mortgage, "because this one will kill you." Years later I learned that she was dying of breast cancer, and that day was one of the last she worked at the bank.

When we feel good, we see guides, guardians, angels all over. When we're down in a hole we don't see them so clearly, but they are there. Step by step I was asked to be a keynoter for a women's conference. A friend suggested I teach story skills at our local university, where I met a trial attorney who suggested I teach his colleagues. One of those attorneys suggested that I sit in on a pre-trial focus group. The attorney whose case was being tested offered to sponsor me as a litigation consultant to a national organization of trial attorneys. I didn't even know such a position – litigation consultant – existed. When that organization called me to consult on cases, other trial attorneys and consultants helped me get up to speed.

This process of recovery took several years. I stayed on at the farm stand while incrementally developing an independent litigation consulting practice that eventually went national. In the 10 years I served as a litigation consultant I helped trial lawyers win tens of millions of dollars on behalf of their plaintiff clients. I found a real calling in that work, and by helping other people I hurt less.

The time came to move to the Pacific Northwest. Like our cedar trees, I am resilient. The therapist who shepherded me through my earlier incest survivor work once told me, "You're like a wolf who gets its foot caught in a trap and will chew it off rather than stay trapped." She didn't know how right she was.

Looking back, it all makes sense. Those 9 months birthed a new me, a consulting practice, a pilgrimage on the Camino de Santiago, a new community, a successful consulting/coaching media production company. What are the chances?

I know this much is true: there are people along the way who show up to give you a hand up. Our job is to recognize that these people have been in the hole, too, and they know the way out. Now it's my turn to show someone else by being my vulnerable, authentic self, peddling hope and imagination to anybody who hears it. That's all any of us want: to know we are seen, heard, understood and of use.

CHAPTER SIX

SELF-CARE /
HEALTH /
WELLNESS

SELF-CARE IS
NOT SELFISH!

"When you care for yourself, others automatically care more for you."

—BYRON EDGINGTON

Have you ever said, "Self-care? I wish I had time for that!" Have you ever said, "I wish I was nicer, calmer, a better listener?" We certainly have, and when we do, it means we haven't taken sufficient time to care for ourselves.

Self-care is something you've got to take time for and practice daily. Like taking a shower, it only works if it's done regularly. You give out only what you have available to give. You can't offer others a drink from an empty glass. You can't even take a drink for yourself from an empty glass. It's too easy these days to work a killer schedule, sleep as little as possible, and neglect your physical and emotional condition. But you're not a machine. You're a beautiful human being with a lot of refreshing drinks to offer when you can. Especially now, with the onslaught of data and information assaulting you every day, it's more important than ever to care for the inner you that's too easily lost.

It becomes too easy as well to listen to the inner voice berating you for thinking you need to step back and practice self-care, when others around you are plodding along, doing the job, watching you take a breather. (A breather. There's a curious expression. We all need to breathe!)

But taking care of yourself should never be shameful or embarrassing. It should be a point of pride. You've seen people who neglect the self-care they should be doing, and they attract more shaming and ridicule than anyone. Maybe watching you care for yourself they'll choose to do likewise. Setting an example can be another reason to practice self-care.

Self-care has no finish line. In other words, until you've taken your last turn around the sun, you need to care for yourself so you can be the amazing person you are. Self-care, like bathing, is a practice that works only when performed daily. Let's explore the various ways you can do self-care, the reasons it's so important, especially now, and what self-care is and is not.

LIKE BATHING, SELF-CARE IS A PRACTICE THAT WORKS ONLY WHEN PERFORMED DAILY

Self-care sounds like a simple concept. You just take care of yourself, right? Yes, that's part of it. The physical and emotional care you need to do to stay healthy, be happy, requires you to do this.

Speaking to ourselves in our minds, our inner dialogue, is normal. We all do it. None of us can identify when the voice changed from cheerleader to critic and belittler. The words we say to ourselves matter, and *you're the only one who controls the voice in your head.*

Why do you allow negative self-talk? You're a success, acknowledge that. You're intelligent, gracious, bright, witty, kind, conscientious, interesting, focused, dedicated. You're an action taker and decision maker. Beginning now, choose to stop criticizing you. It's not only unproductive; it's beneath you. You know who you are. You know where you want to go. You've got what it takes to get there. Own it, and let's get you there.

Will it be easy? No. Breakthroughs rarely are. Ridding yourself of your worst enemy, your inner critic, the creep who calls you an impostor and other nasty, negative things, is mandatory. But you have the power to do it. If you want to silence that voice badly enough, you'll make it happen. You'll find more tips in the guidebook, but here are a few simple ones to start with.

<u>View self-talk as self-care.</u> Write down every positive trait you have.

<u>Be specific.</u> Take ownership of your accomplishments. List them individually, down to the smallest detail.

<u>List your daily activities.</u> How do you treat yourself? What do you do for your immediate and extended family? For friends, coworkers or employees? Keep going, expand on it. When you think you're done, go on to educational and personal development accomplishments, the people you've helped succeed. Don't forget about your volunteer hours, the hand up you offered someone, or the time you paid forward in the drive-through line.

You're not done. There's more. What about the numerous things we do without thinking? They matter, considering how important they are to someone else. That smile you offered someone, the random act of kindness you extended when no one was watching, the $5 you slipped to somebody you thought needed it, the call you made, the testimonial letter you wrote, the event attended that you clearly didn't want to. This is important. You matter. Acknowledge yourself. What you do adds value to others and reminding yourself changes your perception of you.

Now that you're aware of how much value you add to others, it's time to become your own cheerleader. Own it!

But there's more to it than that. There are things you need to avoid as well, things like blaming, shaming, and doubting your own abilities. When your inner critic speaks, put a stop to it. From now on, make it a habit to not give out or receive blame and shame. They're both corrosive in your life and do nothing but drag you down. Self-care is a lot like establishing boundaries, but with a physiological component. There are things that add to your well-being and others that detract from it. Creating a boundary against the latter is good self-care.

Many of us talk about self-care, but few of us take the time or make the effort to do what we ought to do on a regular basis. Many people aren't sure what to do, or even where to begin, especially since their days are already full. One thing we emphasize is this: Self-care is *not* selfish. It's a much-needed practice. You can't give away what you don't have.

In addition to the help offered here, we offer "respite bits," and several other self-care tips in the *Journey Well* guidebook and on our website.

Self-care practices work wonders at centering you, giving you serenity, and silencing the inner critic.

We're committed to the belief that you are amazing, and that your gift is needed, especially now when we're all looking for a better way and expecting to find it. By this point in *Journey Well,* you realize that we mean this; we need all hands on deck these days, all the gifts that you can share. Hiding your gift, hesitant or fearful of sharing it is the opposite of self-care; it's detrimental to our collective serenity. Unwrap your gift through self-care and show it to the world. No matter what it is, we're sure it's amazing.

- You might have a gift for empathy, compassion, or insight to problems many others have.
- You might see things in a different light than anyone else and present your insight in ways others understand and relate to.
- The human eye can detect just 1 percent of the available spectrum of light. That means we don't see 99 percent of the light energy surrounding us. You could be the person who "sees" what others don't.
- You could encourage others to seek self-care for themselves. Recently, the young Olympian Simone Biles opted out of competition for a time. She did this at the apex of her career and to the astonishment of all who knew her. The reaction to her decision was swift and polarizing: People supported her courage. Ms. Biles showed us what self-care truly means, especially for other women.
- Perhaps you're an amazing listener for a troubled friend or family member. Reaching a hand up can give someone a lift, or even save a life.

Simone Biles can be a role model for all of us. By foregoing certain events, Ms. Biles put aside fleeting fame, riches, and the adulation that would certainly have come her way to care for herself. It was her time to shine in the greatest event of all, the ongoing Olympics of self-care and self-respect. When you're receptive to finding this new you, during your chaotic day a quick break can bring about a mental shift, a renewed and needed burst of energy. It can take less than sixty seconds.

We offer you a few simple, easy to do and remember daily practices of self-care, actions that take a few minutes that will make you feel more energized and better about who you are.

A common one is meditation or prayer. It doesn't have to be in silence, alone with a candle, or in a darkened room. You can meditate or pray on a subway or a city bus. You can do either one waiting for your children outside their school. You can meditate while loading the dishwasher, walking in a park, or during an intermission. Mariah's favorite place in the world to meditate was a small stretch of the south coast of Kauai called Mahaulepu. She spent many peaceful and restorative hours there, experiencing the transformative power of the ocean, communing with turtles that seemed to commune with her as well. It was on Kauai that she first heard the message of bringing *Journey Well* to life.

An easy to learn form of meditation is Mindfulness. Here's an example. As you place items in the dishwasher, consider how fortunate you are to have food to stain those plates. Think of the electricity, the water, the mechanical action of the machine that happens with no effort on your part. Focus on the nourishment you and your family have taken from those plates, and how clean they'll soon be again. Some people hand wash dishes or pack their kids' lunches as a form of soothing meditation.

Here's another list of self-care techniques:

- Meditation: Meditating takes commitment, so start slow and practice every day. It doesn't have to be time-consuming to be effective. You can also do "guided" meditation.

- Aromatherapy: This is essential oils diffusing into the air, spreading the aroma through your home. Put the essential oil on cotton pads to smell, or for use in the shower turning your bath into a mini-spa treatment.

- Reiki: Find a practitioner or learn self-reiki. This ancient practice is one of the best relaxation and healing arts ever devised.

- Prayer for many people is good self-care. Depending on your beliefs and understandings, praying to a higher power—the universe, or whatever god you recognize—can center you.

- Gratitude Journaling: Writing what you're grateful for is self-care that helps you appreciate all you've been given, including the power to express gratitude. In the guidebook and at the website, you'll find a template for gratitude journaling.

- Spa/Massage: Pampering yourself with massage has always been exquisite self-care. It's not selfish to indulge in a massage session; it shows that you value yourself.

- Breathing exercises: These are simple, effective, convenient, and non-intrusive. And you can do them anywhere. Breathing exercises truly are "inspiring."

- Sleep: Getting sufficient sleep is self-care, not an indulgence or selfishness. Time asleep has long-term health benefits such as reduced stress, lower blood pressure, better long-term health, and a better attitude. Few of us get enough sleep these nights.

- Self Journaling: Writing about your accomplishments and activities can be self-care. The act of writing what you do well and the wins you've had, the value you've added to someone else's life, the brighter and better plan for your future life, all that is self-care because it puts your positive energy into the world for everyone, or just for the most important person, you.

- Paying forward: Recognizing what you've been given can raise your sense of self-worth. Pay for the toll fee for the car behind you or the family at the restaurant. Pay for the older couple's meal anonymously. Give the barista a twenty for your eleven-dollar latte and muffin and leave the change. The warm feeling you'll get is your brain releasing the "feel-good" chemicals.

- Mirror work to include the "I love you" messages.

- Affirmations: Sending warm wishes to others is self-care as well. Praising yourself and others for a wonderful job, recognizing small successes, makes you feel good as well. In affirming others, you're claiming your own value.

- Nutrition: The food you eat is a big indicator of your self-care. Find a meal plan that keeps you healthy and energetic.
- *Receiving* affirmations: This is self-care that's seldom noted.

It's hard to learn to receive. If you don't *get* very well you can't *give* very well. Self-care dictates that the ability to receive is vital. Without claiming your value there can be no "self" in self-care.

One of the most neglected self-care exercises is one you can do in your sleep. That's because it <u>is</u> sleep. According to Arianna Huffington, in her book *The Sleep Revolution*, sleep is *one of humanity's great unifiers. It binds us to one another, to our ancestors, to our past, and to the future.* Ms. Huffington goes on to claim that "this relationship (with sleep) is in crisis. If you type *why am I so?* into Google, the first suggestion is *why am I so tired?* According to *ScienceDaily*, sleep loss costs the US economy more than $400 billion dollars every year.

So, the immediate question everyone has is, how much sleep do you need? Huffington's book debunks the idea of the overachiever's mastery of their world getting by on four or five hours of sleep per night. A rough rule of thumb is to split your allotted twenty-four hours in three parts: eight hours for work, eight hours for sleep, and eight hours for whatever else you choose.

"Sleep that knits up the ravell'd sleeve of care,
...Chief nourisher in life's feast."
—WILLIAM SHAKESPEARE *MACBETH*

From *The Sleep Revolution*, here's a scientific scale of how much sleep you need, depending on your age.

— Pre-schoolers 10 to 13 hours

— Teenagers 8 to 10 hours

— Young Adults 7 to 9 hours

— Adults 7 to 9 hours

— Older adults 7 to 8 hours

And, of course, there are suggestions for how to obtain sleep, what to wear, what to do and not do in bed, how to prepare for bedtime, and foods and beverages to avoid prior to sleep.

Too many of us believe we can get by with less. Sleep loss does more than fill in the Google search parameter and trigger the algorithm. It drags you down, makes you less attentive, lowers your quality of life, and can even decrease the length of your life.

Do you recall who taught you about self-care as a child? Likely no one, but it's never too late to begin. Once you decide to venture down the self-care path, you'll be amazed at the changes. Initially, you'll find roadblocks and detours. People may question your new focus. Others might wonder what's wrong with you. Some will be curious, kind, and questioning, perhaps wishing to undertake the same for themselves. If you stick with the journey to self-care, you'll come to a bend in the road and make a magnificent turn that reveals a new you, one previously unknown, a new you we're certain you'll love and cherish.

When you begin to treat yourself with kindness and respect, those traits naturally influence others. Your life will change in profound ways, going in a direction you always knew was possible.

TAKING CARE OF YOURSELF FIRST MEANS YOU UNDERSTAND THE VALUE OF SELF-CARE

SELF-CARE FOR HEALTHCARE WORKERS

The COVID crisis is the major driver of healthcare workers' overwhelming anxiety right now. This section of *Journey Well, You Are More Than Enough* is aimed at our former colleagues—nurses, physicians, med-techs, LPNs, RTs, PTs, hospital and clinic staff, all pre-hospital workers, Air-Med Pilots, Flight RNs, EMTs and EMTPs—who serve in every capacity during this awful time. We hope this part of the book, and sections in the guidebook, relieve some of the stress you're facing.

If you're looking for support, empathy, understanding, and tools to help you attend to your own needs, we get that. Here are self-care methods you can use while tending to the healthcare needs of others. By the way, we've always admired you and your dedication. That level of admiration is now through the roof. Thank you for all you do.

Let's start with bullying. It's been said of nursing staff that they eat their young, but this is no time to give credence to that reputation. If you have young, fresh-out-of-school nurses, please treat them with the respect they deserve. Instead of bullying them when they make mistakes, reach out and teach them. It's a lot to ask with the load you're carrying at present, but your instinct is to help so listen to that.

When you're overwhelmed, too stressed to be effective, and feeling like you can't go on, ask about in-house stress resources, find a support group, start your own, look out for each other.

When you hear the inner critic telling you you're failing, that you're a fraud, that soon they'll discover your incompetence, remember this: You're not a fraud, you're a well-trained, highly credentialed healthcare practitioner. You made it through school, passed your boards—which was no easy feat—obtained additional certifications, and have no blemishes in your record. You're very good at what you do, so learn to silence that obnoxious voice in your head. Here's how: Give yourself affirmations. Tell yourself what you've done, where you've been posted, the difference you've made to patients and their families. Remember one patient you had enormous success with. Envision that person, see their family, enter their room, and see them smile at you. Go with them to the curb as they get in the family car and go home. Give yourself a hug because *they* would. You're very good at what you do, never forget that.

If you hear of a colleague struggling, listen to them. Take five minutes and talk them down. Don't offer solutions, just listen. Hold their hand. Look in their eyes. Make them understand that you're really hearing them. If you're the one needing help, don't be afraid to ask for it.

Look up our 60-second respites in the guidebook. Here's an abbreviated list of them.

- Essential oils: Obtain a vial of lavender. Put a few drops on a cotton pad, stuff it into your scrubs where you can smell it. Take deep breaths from it and allow the calming power of the lavender to refresh you.
- Breathwork: Simple deep breathing exercises can be extremely helpful in lowering stress, reducing heart rate, calming you, and bringing a bit of self-care when you need it most.
- Self-affirmation: As discussed above, remind yourself how far you've come, how hard you worked to get the position you hold, and how well you've done the job. Whatever follows I AM... follows you. So quiet your jumbled thoughts and your anxiety with the I AM exercise: I AM...extremely competent—a valued member of the team—really smart—very knowledgeable—always reliable—highly respected.
- I CAN: Use a variation of the exercise above and substitute I CAN. I Can—start IVs when no one else can—

sense when a patient is about to crash—explain procedures so patients understand them—tell families exactly what they need to know—translate what the doctor just told them.

- Go the f**k to sleep: Sleep loss costs the US economy $4 billion dollars a year. A lot of that loss is likely in the healthcare profession. Contrary to what a lot of people think, we do not function well on only four or five hours of sleep a night. Don't be a hero. Unless your job is in imminent peril, take the time for adequate sleep, and not in the break room. Check our sleep tips in the guidebook and take care of yourself in the best way there is, by getting enough rest.

- Do CPR—Caring Personal Rescue: Make a tent with your fingers. Press each fingertip into its opposite. Close your eyes, take steady breaths, and feel the pulses in your fingers. This will slow your heart rate, lower blood pressure, and fill you with calm.

The stupid inner voice starts yakking when you get hungry, tired, and frustrated at the worst possible times. Learn to silence it by using the techniques above because you don't need the extra burden right now, or ever.

Find whatever self-care works for you and then find the time to use it regularly. It will keep you healthy and allow you to keep doing the job you love. We miss the profession every day, so we're with you. Thanks again for what you do.

Become present with what self-care offers you. The opportunity to clear your thoughts, to be open to the energy flowing through you, giving you a sense of peace. Quietly, with a breath in and a breath out, notice it all, your life in all its amazing dimensions, its vivid colors, its gentle breezes bringing new blessings if you're willing to receive them.

Practicing self-care should be a part of your daily routine. Imagine if your spouse or one of your children worked as hard as you do, day after day, leaving their health and wellness aside. You'd eventually intervene in some way, in a subtle or not so subtle fashion. Why do you allow yourself to disregard self-care for you?

Not enough time? Feeling selfish? Don't know where to start? Or you don't want another chore added to your already hectic day? We get that. But look at the long-term view. If you're settled into a career, and enjoy what you do, it's likely you'll stay at it for many years. Plan to retire with lots of energy, opportunities, and ambition. Self-care now establishes a routine that will help you get there.

For those who are so exhausted and overwhelmed that you just want out, be gentle with yourself. Take some time. Consider counseling to help you make good decisions around this.

Self-care time is never wasted time. It's critical if you seek the better and brighter world you want. Thank you and journey well.

HERE ARE THREE IMPORTANT POINTS FROM THIS CHAPTER:

★ You can't take care of others unless you care for yourself.

★ Especially now, with the onslaught of data and information assaulting you every day, it's more important than ever to care for the inner you that's too easily lost.

★ Self-care is *not* selfish. It's a much-needed practice. You can't give away what you don't have.

ACTION STEPS:

≈ Stay off social media for a day, a week, or a month! Take a "radical sabbatical," as our friends Dennis and Ali call it.

≈ Ignore Facebook, Twitter, Instagram, LinkedIn, and other forms of digital dopamine that hold you hostage.

≈ Place drop of lavender oil on a cotton pad and smell it a few times a day taking deep breaths.

≈ Use lavender as a hand or foot massage. Lavender has calming and healing properties.

≈ Get more sleep! You can't function at 100 percent if your sleep bank is at 50 percent. Sleep isn't a luxury, it's critically important to self-care.

PERSONAL JOURNEY

LAURA STALEY

"Passionately supporting people thriving | Founder of Cherish Your World | Author of *Abundant Heart, Live Inspired* | Columnist and featured contributing writer BizCatalyst360° | Columnist OWL Magazine | Sacred Stories Blog."

Laura Staley Ph.D. is the author of recently published *Abundant Heart: Thoughts on Healing, Loving, and Living Free.*

Recently Laura Staley posted dance videos on social media to inspire contributions to Kaleidoscope Youth Center. It was as part of her passionate commitment, an enduring vision to live in a world where children are seen, heard, believed, cherished, and nurtured with loving kindness into adulthood.

https://www.kycohio.org

~

CARE TO GO BEYOND

As a full time parent of two small children, I often woke up in the morning wondering if someone would finally ask me, "How may I help you?" Intellectually, I knew I needed to be all in for my children. Developmentally, they could do some things for themselves, but in the very early years, not too many. Emotionally, I felt twinges of resentment for my unmet, aching needs left over from a difficult childhood.

I knew parenting aligned with my heart, contained a path to healing, to transformation. I passionately wanted my children to feel cherished, accepted, unburdened. I wanted them to spend whole days in their PJs, to build forts with blankets and chairs, to play make believe, and discover the many joys of the natural world.

Self-care seemed like a foreign concept, a good idea in an alternate reality. I'd steeped in the hot messages of selfishness. I knew silent martyrdom, selflessness, and unhealthy people pleasing. I'd gotten excellent training from volatile, impossible adult expectations, a dark version of Cinderella's nightmarish life.

The idea of self-care felt shameful, indulgent, and yet, when avoided, I noticed I became steeped with resentment, which became a distraction, a disempowerment to my genuine core commitment of loving service to my family. Once I connected with my sense of agency to care for myself from the inside out, I became more effective and genuinely joyous when caring for others.

Carving out moments for myself when my children were young, I mustered courage that seemed like defiance. I claimed a table in a room as my spot for journaling, a chair in the master bedroom as my peace chair. A few years later I felt fortunate to have a whole room. These spaces contributed to my sense of having a separate self. I felt glimmers of worthiness inside as shame and resentments slowly dissipated.

I time blocked my daily schedule for writing, reading, and pondering. I began to rewire my life to include my essential self, to hold compassionate space for my younger selves, who had gotten very little respite from demands to perform, perfect, and please.

Once I experienced the benefits of hiring a quality babysitter for my children and taking a few moments of downtime, I became a happier, more centered mom.

As my children got older, I signed up for a yoga class every Wednesday night. What a haven this became in my week. My family noticed the shift and got excited for me to attend yoga class. I also participated in a Meditate, Activate, Integrate (MAI) class facilitated by a gifted, cherished friend.

In MAI, I experienced various meditation practices. We joyously danced, crafted, and journaled. The MAI class became the foundation for my self-care practices I continue to this day.

Conscious, healthy parenting remains a most difficult job.

Because some of us choose to rupture the abuse cycle, reparent ourselves at the same time we parent our children, resentments can still leak out as a signal for self-care. Healing outdated patterns takes committed fresh practices and courage.

Self-care becomes a foundation for healthy interactions with the most important people in your life. Reframing self-care as essential to your effectiveness, you notice you have even more energy and focus. By taking care of you, you can radiate a centered place of love which touches everyone you encounter. You are worth it. More important than your words or deeds is your energy presence.

May you engage self-care practices which fill your heart, body, and soul. May this important investment uplift your contribution to others and our world.

CHAPTER SEVEN

BURN THE BAGGAGE / FREEDOM

FIRE IS CLEANSING. WHAT RISES FROM THE ASHES IS ENERGY

"You're not on this earth just to survive;
you're here to thrive, to serve, to create, and to be happy."
—MARIAH EDGINGTON

We mentioned in a previous chapter that we had plans for your baggage, that is, a way for you to dispose of it properly. Now that you've unpacked the heavy weights and made tough decisions on what to keep, what to use as steppingstones, and what to discard, it's time to work the plan. We call it *luggage* for a reason: we lug it around all our lives, often without thinking and not realizing that we can choose to get rid of it. This chapter is titled Burn the Baggage for a reason.

In the companion guidebook for *Journey Well, You Are More than Enough*, we include a section to write down past missteps, the burdens you carry, and difficult events in your past. We suggest you add a few things to that list, items that remind you of those times, those events, and perhaps those toxic people from your past. Maybe you'd like to include photographs, souvenirs, or ticket stubs from those times, or an old diary that lists things that dredge the bad stuff up. Include household items, old newspaper clippings, maybe a school yearbook from a class that caused you pain and embarrassment. We want you to release painful memories from abuse and trauma situations if you're able to. You could write letters to people who've hurt you or about events that caused you pain.

Collect those items, look at them as reminders of a you that no longer exists. Then go camping where there's a fire pit, visit a state park with a fire stand, or use your patio grill and burn them up. You could hold a "Burn the Baggage" party. Create a *Journey Well* book club and hold a group burn. Invite other people who affirmed you in your journey and those who entered your new life to come along, replacing those who've fallen away. Make it an event. Ask friends and family if they'd like to do their own unpacking and join in as you burn the baggage together. Watch those burning letters you wrote turn to ashes and see them waft away on the wind.

Fire is cleansing. It's also energy. Burning the baggage empowers you and cleanses your life of the rubbish of useless memories. It can be your version of Burning (Wo)man, with a twist. Mark it on your calendar and create a Burn the Baggage party. (Why is there no annual Burning Woman event? You should create one.)

Some people may feel awkward doing the incineration activity. Some may ridicule the simplicity of it or dismiss it as childish or useless. But what you focus on expands, and if your focus is on positive, affirming things, those things will expand, and the flame from your baggage-burning exercise will bring light and warmth to you. It can also generate a commitment to self-care, eliminating negative paradigms, and putting positive new habits in place.

SEEK OUT PEOPLE WHO FAN THE FLAMES OF YOUR PASSION

We do this to celebrate those who are prepared to accept the simple message we offer: You are <u>More</u> than enough. You're not on this earth just to survive; you're here to thrive, to serve, to create, and to be happy. There are many reasons to burn the baggage, but this is certainly an important one. You need this self-care for you.

We can't overstress this. You have a gift we all need. Your gift must be sent out into the world, up from the ashes of all that baggage, and distributed freely. Your *one wild and precious life* must include taking what you learned, and what you know, and giving it away. Serving others is the best way to secure the riches of your own contentment. Giving = Living.

TRYING TO TAKE OFF WITH TOO MUCH BAGGAGE
WEIGHT, WON'T ALLOW YOU TO RISE

Allow yourself to release the past and move forward, burning the baggage as a building block to a better, brighter future. Building that new life on the cold ashes of your past says you're already stronger and more resilient.

One way to burn the baggage and to move into the next wonderful phase of your life is to establish a great goal. Here's a shocking statistic taken from a recent poll at Harvard University. Unbelievably, eighty-three percent of the alumni questioned had NO goals! These were some of the most intelligent and gifted members of society, yet when polled about their personal and professional goals, they had no answer.

Unless you're working toward a goal that gets you out of bed every morning, a goal that drives you to excel at everything you do, you'll wander around lost and unhappy. An empty piece of luggage has lots of room that can be filled with better things.

Here's an analogy about baggage from my aviation days. By design, configuration, and engineering, all aircraft have certain capacities, capabilities, and limits. One of those limits is the weight they're designed to carry. Every aircraft has a load limit, a weight beyond which it won't fly. Since gravity is equally and constantly present for everything, it doesn't matter how big an aircraft is or how powerful its engines are. Every aircraft has a weight limit.

Our lives are like that too. When you try taking off with too much baggage weight, it simply won't allow you to rise. To facilitate your takeoff, you need to burn the baggage. You've heard the expression lighten up. This is a pure definition of it. To take off and soar, you need to lighten up and take off unencumbered.

EVERYTHING IS A CHOICE, SO MAKE *YOURSELF* YOUR FIRST CHOICE

Burning your baggage can also warm you and chase away those who try to douse your enthusiasm. Distancing yourself from those who bring negativity into your life, and setting boundaries with them, improves your self-esteem. You're not required to continue an unhealthy relationship. Everything is a choice, so make *yourself* your first choice. Remember what you read about boundaries. A good friend can be better than an old friend.

Speaking to women reading this, here's a subject that must be addressed, as sad as it is. The heaviest baggage women and girls carry is often the judgments of other women. For whatever reason, some women can't abide the possibility of other women succeeding. Throughout history, the pattern shows women challenging other women, instead of joining together to find common ground and shared success.

You've been aware of this conundrum since junior high. Whatever initiatives come along to benefit girls and women, the biggest opponents of it are often other women. Is it jealousy? Is it anxiety over appearances? Do women and girls who battle other women's advancement feel threatened when a woman succeeds, reverting to the old, tired, zero-sum mentality?

A CANDLE LOSES NOTHING BY LIGHTING ANOTHER CANDLE

Whatever the reason, you must learn to ignore those forces of female resistance and push on. As heartbreaking as it might be, you may have to separate yourself from women who have been long-time friends if they refuse to support you or try to diminish your accomplishments.

This is baggage that needs to be in the hottest part of the fire. This impediment serves no practical value. It actively detracts from your efforts to succeed. Your past events and missteps can be easily dismissed. They can't be fixed or changed in any case. But headwinds from other women and girls is an ongoing, and unnecessary limitation. If you're going to journey well, you'll need to bypass that detour.

Your life is so important. Remember, if you don't yet believe in *you*, then lean on us, because we believe in YOU. As you burn the baggage and warm your hands in the fire's golden glow, here are a few positive steps to help you move beyond the ashes.

> We want you to succeed. We've created a Facebook page where you can share your wins.
> https://www.facebook.com/groups/1245811645906933.

≋ Creating a community of supportive people allows you to tap into other people's expertise. Those who've preceded you, and have the ashes to show for it, now enjoy helping you. Reach out to them and share the story of your journey-well experience.

≋ Paying it forward is a big part of the *Journey Well* message. As exciting as it is to hear of your success, it's even more so knowing you've helped others succeed. That's the definition of a good life.

≋ The word synergy means cooperating with others so the whole is greater than its parts. Burning your baggage allows that to happen, giving you resources you didn't know you had, increasing your contribution to our collective effort.

≋ Provide resources to your community, not just another person, and not just for yourself. Especially in this uncertain time, it's too easy for you to cling to your baggage like it's a lifesaving device. Expand your vision. Look at the width and the depth of your world, its astonishing size, and the possibilities available to you. There are more options to serve than hours in the day.

≋ You may want to consider doing what Mariah did. She found a community of people who raise each other up and celebrate their wins on a regular basis. Within the wonderful LinkedIn platform, she's nurtured a sizable following. If you're on LinkedIn, join her there. If you're not, create an account and follow like-minded people on a positive platform.

linkedin.com/in/mariahedgington

HERE ARE THREE IMPORTANT POINTS FROM THIS CHAPTER:

★ Fire is cleansing. Burning the baggage empowers you and cleanses your life of useless memories.

★ Use the past as building blocks or fertilizer for a new garden!

★ The heaviest baggage women and girls carry is often the judgments of other women.

ACTION STEPS:

≋ Take an old piece of luggage and fill it with pages of bad or painful memories. Find a fire pit or outside grill and burn it up!

≋ Form a *Journey Well* Burn the Baggage Facebook group or other supportive community.

≋ Take pictures of your burning baggage and post them in Facebook and Instagram.

≋ Frame the photo and hang it in a prominent spot.

PERSONAL JOURNEY

BRAD BURCHNELL

"Chief Heartset Life Coach, and Founder of From My Heart to Yours, LLC."

Brad Burchnell's story reflects the desire to burn baggage that no longer assists his journey, and to recover from the tragedy of his daughter's suicide. Burning the Baggage is rarely easy, but often necessary. Here's Brad's version of it.

～

You start taking a hard look at who you are as a person, defining what your hurts are, what you really know about *you*, and start identifying that, journaling, writing. A big component of it was writing letters to those who hurt me. That really helped, especially with all my family issues, and the suicide of my daughter.

Doing that is cathartic, because when you end up looking at it, you force yourself to look at who you really are, and that's a moment you'll never get back. As you look at yourself...you start reframing, rebuilding acceptance for yourself. Your healing journey comes with self-compassion, self-love, self-forgiveness. That's a major portion of healing of the heart, soul, and spirit.

I was talking about this to my boss a month ago, and the first thing he said was, you know it's been about a year, how do you feel? I said I feel great, I have the most peace I've ever had. Being at peace, and being able to smile again, I feel happy most every morning. It's very rare that I'm unhappy. My practice is pretty consistent: I get up, go to my basement which is also my gym, with a candle I keep a low light, and I put on some spiritual music. I meditate while walking on the treadmill for half an hour. It helps from the standpoint of starting and finishing the same way every day. I also do gratitude journaling.

It becomes a real challenge, because people fool themselves, saying I'm doing great, and doing fine. I said that for a long time. Part of the problem comes from masculinity...because we (men) have a lack of trust in vulnerability. We see it as weakness. Exploring my core values was really understanding what makes me uniquely me. It's been good for me going through this part where I'm by myself, especially as we're going into my least favorite time of the year in Michigan.

Every day I make a choice to be happy. I still have bad days, but they're not nearly as bad or long as they used to be. Attention-grabbing people do the floodlighting for effect to overshare, and I was doing that. Last year was bad, because I was in pain, and didn't know how to control it.

Then I started journaling. If you generate it outward, and write it down, also sharing it with somebody that's worthy of sharing it with, sometimes it's not even your best friend. Sometimes it's someone that will provide that safe space, not be judgmental. It's a difficult balance. There are people who the first thing they do is say 'why would you do that?' Or which is worse. 'oh you poor thing...' That's pouring gasoline on the fire.

My friend R is making decisions right now too. I told her, here's a practice I learned from a friend of mine, Mariah. R, do you look in the mirror? She goes, *of course.* I said, do you tell yourself affirmations? She said *like what?* I said, well this isn't like little girls in a mirror saying *I love my mom, I love dad, my hair looks great.* It's looking in the mirror saying *I appreciate you; I appreciate where you came from; I love you.* The lesson I've learned is that you're the author of your own life. You get to choose what your ending looks like, and if you don't choose, it will be chosen for you.

CHAPTER EIGHT

VISIONEERING

THINK FROM THE END
TO CREATE THE LIFE
YOU DESERVE

"Whatever possessions you have now were once your thoughts."
—BYRON EDGINGTON

W hy are we all so inhibited in a way, so unable to open our vision to allow new worlds and new possibilities? One reason is fear, your hesitation to change what appears comfortable and familiar. That makes sense. We're all afraid of something, and change is one of the most common universal fears. So, you're in good company. But let's explore this a bit further and look at how your resistance to change and new ideas can hold you back. Visioneering is a tool that gives you the power to do that. If your mind can be more open, more accepting of the wonders available to you, the better, brighter world you crave can be yours for the taking.

Visioneering is just a fancy word for what some refer to as thinking from the end, the method we suggest for you to create the better and brighter life for yourself. Here's why you should do this and how it works:

First, we offer what seems like a radical idea. There are no inventions, only discoveries. Here's what we mean. Everything that's ever been or ever will be available to us is already here. The wheel, agriculture, bronze tools, money, sailing ships, and cities—all these things were once unimagined, yet today they're taken for granted. We can't imagine a world without them. No agriculture? No metal tools? No cities? Impossible.

A THOUGHT CAN NEVER BE DISMISSED. YOU CANNOT UNTHINK SOMETHING

Reach in your pocket and touch your smartphone. It's an amazing tool, isn't it? In addition to its function as a phone, it's your camera, notation device, email portal, game platform, messaging system, and a myriad of other tools, right in your hand.

Not too many years ago, the smartphone was a dream. Then someone had the idea that all those tools should be available to you in one place, and that place should be your hand. That vision shimmered into view, becoming the smartphone you're holding now. Today you take the device for granted. Whatever comes along in the next generation will likewise be taken for granted, and the next thing, and the next. So why not imagine your better and brighter life right now as well?

Envision that better life for yourself today. A world of plenty, compassion, love, support, and acceptance. A world in which you take sustenance, shelter, and safety for granted. Imagine your world of gentleness and understanding, where equality is a given. Imagine that better world for yourself. Then keep this in mind: It's already here, and you can imagine it into reality.

See your new life filled with joy, contentment, love, and understanding. See your daily life as a joyful, productive passage of days caring for yourself and serving others. Envision waking to the gentle sound of your favorite music, the aroma of coffee brewing, the breeze fresh with the tang of overnight rain. While you're doing this exercise, you're visioneering. You're describing a better world for yourself and everyone else, and those ideas are entering your mind, filling it with pleasant and generous thoughts. You're visioneering. And you're getting better at it as you go.

The human mind absorbs whatever input you add to it from stimuli that come to you constantly. On any given day, you'll add hundreds of thousands of inputs, images, ideas, and thoughts. Those inputs must go somewhere, and where they go is into the recesses of your mind, to create whatever reality you allow and whatever you've chosen to become important. Whatever possessions you have now were once just thoughts.

A thought can never be dismissed. You cannot *unthink* something. And if you can think it, you can achieve it. Whatever you have in your midst at present was once just a thought until you imagined its utility and brought it forth in physical form. That also applies to the better and brighter world you imagine.

Hold what you DO want, the future you want to live in and be part of. Hold it in your mind. Dream it, imagine it, and create it mentally, and be very focused on specific parts of it. Review it often. We journal about what we want twice daily. And my friend, you're holding in your hand one of our dreams, a *New York Times* best-selling book!

Apply this concept to the life and happiness you wish to have. Visioneer the yet to be *discovered* ways you can bring whatever it is you desire into your life. Do you want more money? A better vehicle? Better access to food, friends, or family? Do you want a better job, higher position, or more captivating opportunities? Do you want better health, a better understanding of your children or spouse? Visioneer those things, and with focused attention and necessary actions, they'll be yours.

We don't wish to suggest that this is easy, or a finger snap away. But these things are available to you if you can visioneer them. What you focus on expands. When you believe that seemingly trite expression, you'll understand that what you have in your life right now, today, was once what you focused on. The home you live in, your current job, your spouse and children, the vehicle you drive. All these things were once in your imagination and are now present in your life.

There are no accidents in the universe, no mistakes. You once were without what you have, and it's yours now. It didn't arrive out of the blue. You thought it there, and you can think better and brighter things going forward.

Focus fully on what you want. Be specific. Don't imagine "a new car." Imagine a brand new, red Toyota Corolla with paddle shifters, six-speed manual transmission, and a rear spoiler. Smell the new-car aroma as you open the driver side door and ease behind the wheel. Pull your new cherry-red Corolla into your garage and notice the neighbor watching you. Envision stepping out of the car and waving to him. Is that fun or what? Notice we didn't say, "won't that be fun?" We used present tense. "Is that fun or what?"

Don't just imagine having more money. Imagine taking the envelope with found money out of your mailbox. Envision the company logo in the transparent window. Envision slitting the envelope open and seeing the figure, $6,000.00! It's a refund from an old insurance policy your family canceled years ago. Visioneer taking your family on vacation to Maui with that money.

Don't just wish for a new job or a different career. Envision accepting an executive vice president's position at a Fortune Fifty, with a corner office, two personal secretaries, and a desk with no drawers. Not having drawers in your desk is a sure sign you've arrived. The reason we don't get what we want is because we don't know what we want. And often this means we don't know what to ask for or imagine, or we're fearful of asking for whatever reason.

With a nod to an idea proposed by Jack Canfield of *The Success Principles*, one way to decide what you want is to list twenty things you want to do, twenty things you want to have, and twenty things you want to be. Another way is a fun exercise, asking a friend to help you make your I want list. Again, be specific. Don't just wish for a new car, more money, a house on the beach. Specify what make, model, and year of car, exactly how much money, and what size house you want on which specific stretch of beach. Look for more details on doing this in the *Journey Well* guidebook.

Create a vision board. Take a poster-size panel and hang it on your wall. When you see things in magazines you crave, cut the pictures out and paste them on your vision board. Create the better, brighter life you want right there in front of you. If you can hold it in your head, you can hold it in your hand. Look over your vision board every day, and when the things you've pasted there begin to arrive in your life, as they certainly will, check them off one by one.

As a variation of this, purchase a blank notebook and create a "wins" book for yourself. When you succeed at something, or when your vision board pays off with that new red Toyota, write it in your wins book. No one else needs to know of these tools, but they work, and when you start visioneering the things you want, you'll be amazed at how quickly it happens.

One reason we don't get what we want is what we call the trap of comfort and facility. As counterintuitive as it sounds, it's much easier to imagine abundance and prosperity if you're destitute. In modern society, surrounded by convenience, ease, and facility, it's difficult to justify wanting better, higher, and more. It feels selfish. Of course, just because you own a lot of material things doesn't mean you're happy or fulfilled. It can mean the opposite. Retail therapy is a thing. Many people indulge in it to counter the pain of empty lives.

Many will say this visioneering idea is a pipe dream, that it can't happen. People who say that are right; it can't happen for them because they've already shut the door to it. If you believe you'll never see it—you'll never see it. Pretty simple.

We don't suggest that anyone impoverish themselves to feel better. As Teyve said in *Fiddler on the Roof,* "There's no shame in being poor, but it's no great honor either!" We're promoting better and brighter tomorrows, even if it means shedding material things you once couldn't live without. Visioneering also allows you to bring transcendence into existence, and that's a definition of a great life.

VISIONEERING IS TO HELP YOU FIND A BETTER LIFE

The concern can be well founded if you've never been happy with what you have. If you're one of those people who crave whatever you see, and your desire for more, bigger, faster, flashier, and better things is what drives you, then this exercise may not work for you. The purpose of visioneering is to help you find a better life, and the richer experience that's evaded you for a long time. A life of comfort can be a trap. It can paralyze you and kill your desire for a better life, because moving past what you already have might mean giving that comfort up for a time.

It's a choice. If your level of satisfaction in life is low, despite the material items you're surrounded with, then visioneering a better, brighter life and starting anew could be the best thing you've ever done for yourself as you set out to journey well.

Visioneering can be either an active process, like the exercise you performed above, or it can be passive. You can silence your mind, find a quiet spot even in a busy, noisy place, and allow your vision to come to you. Let your thoughts roam and ramble, and new ideas and perspectives appear faster than you can imagine. It will excite you to know that whatever thoughts and ideas you have while you're doing this really can become your reality. In the guidebook and in the online course we expand on the idea of the competitive vs the creative mind. Suffice to say that modern life is not conducive to our creative minds.

Here's another consideration in the visioneering exercise, another aspect of it: intuition. This visioneering tool relies on experience and to a certain extent on time. Age and personal exposure to some things can give you stronger and more immediate access to intuition, and the results can be amazing. Byron knows exactly how this works.

Here's an example from my days in the cockpit. One morning, I was flying along above power poles on a job that required me to count those poles and mark them with GPS equipment. The sun was just cresting, and I was flying due east directly into its yellow glare. My two passengers were busy with their counting and marking equipment.

As I cruised through a narrow valley, following the line of poles, I kept the helicopter lined up at just the right altitude and airspeed. Suddenly, I noticed a lone power pole perched atop the ridge to my right. At that moment my intuition kicked in, the sense I'd gained over many years, telling me there was danger.

I slowed the helicopter, stopped at a hover, and scanned across to the left side of the ridge. My intuition had told me that the pole I'd seen had to have a mate somewhere, and that its power line had to connect those poles. I looked across to the opposite ridge, and sure enough there was another power pole. So, where was the line between them?

I peered ahead into the glare. And there it was, not fifty feet in front of me, a strand of wires directly across my flight path. Had I continued flying, disregarding the intuitive sense of alarm inside my head, I would have flown into them. Many helicopter accidents happen when pilots hit wires.

Visioneering isn't just an active practice that you must clear your mind and calendar to do. It means being open to the messages and vibrations around you, the alarms that go off when your sense of danger or opportunity rings. This intuitive sense gets better and stronger with practice and with paying attention and heeding its message.

Today, before any more time passes, create a vision board for your imagined new life. Start cutting and pasting the things and events you want. Get a win book and start filling its pages with the successes that will come. Visioneer your new life, one day at a time, one hour at a time. You deserve it, and visioneering will bring it to you. It's the best way there is to journey well.

HERE ARE THREE IMPORTANT POINTS FROM THIS CHAPTER:

★ There are no inventions, only discoveries.

★ Envision a better life for yourself. A world of plenty, compassion, love, support, and acceptance are waiting for you.

★ What you focus on expands.

ACTION STEPS:

≋ Look at the devices you own, your smartphone, car, kitchen utensils, computers, TV, and expand on each one's impact on your life.

≋ Stretch the purpose of those things and imagine different uses for them.

≋ Envision yourself as the creator of a new technology, purpose, or method.

PERSONAL JOURNEY

ALI AND DENNIS PITOCCO

With a writer in every port, too young for crossword puzzles, and not interested in pickleball, Ali and Dennis Pitocco retired, looking for ways to use their "time, talent, and treasure" to help others. BizCatalyst 360°, The Friendship Bench, GoodWorks.com, and other initiatives are the result of their efforts. Their contribution to this chapter on visioneering was a no brainer.

~~~

(On retirement) we had to make decisions. How do you want to spend your time? Having been economically blessed with the sale of our UK Business, we settled into Tampa Bay with choices to be made. Akin to the dog who's been chasing the car for years, we "caught the car" –now what do we do with it?

We were too young to do crossword puzzles, not interested in playing pickleball (at least not till they change the name). So, we took our time, and took some long walks to decide what was most important to us, as we recognized just how blessed we were to have such choices at a relatively young age. In the end, we decided to carve our commitment into three things – giving back (not just writing a check, but investing our time, our talent, and our treasure), intentional travel (across the world before across the USA) and keeping our minds sharp.

Well, our *intentional* travels have been relatively non-stop for the past fifteen years (slowed only by the pandemic restrictions). By intentional, we mean traveling on purpose to where we really want to go, versus our years of business travel where our sightseeing was virtually limited to airports, taxis, and meeting rooms. And with a focus on discovering the rest of the world BEFORE discovering America. As we've learned over the years, it's amazing how we view the evening news through a different lens, having personally visited many of the countries mentioned in the context of news.

Along the way, "keeping our minds sharp" took the form of launching BizCatalyst 360°, and our "giving back" commitment has flourished as well – evolving as not only a "roll-up-your-sleeves" commitment to Meals on Wheels of Tampa Bay (delivering meals, volunteering in their offices, serving on their Board as Chair) over the past decade, but ultimate launch of GoodWorks 360° – our global nonprofit consulting foundation – in business to sustain nonprofits worldwide via pro bono advisory services –all delivered through our now-established network of circa four dozen professionals worldwide.

(Speaking of visioneering) it wasn't like there was a business plan for BizCatalyst 360° (or for that matter,

GoodWorks 360°), there never has been, it just evolved day after day –driven by so many amazing connections we've made along the way. From a publishing perspective, we crafted it all starting with what was best for our writers and our audience –casting aside all the classic industry standards, expectations, and roadblocks hampering freedom of expression. And unlike virtually all other media operations, everything we do is "for good" versus "for profit" allowing us (along with our writers) to simply spread our collective wings in whatever direction that matters.

In recent years, our media operations have grown to the point that everything is now tucked under 360° Nation, enveloping BizCatalyst 360°, GoodWorks 360°, and 360 Nation Studios –taking our "for good" commitment into the world of live and streaming global events.

Taking a look back, we've had a number of "aha" moments and discoveries, all of which inspired us to simply dig deeper and reach farther to make a difference. Of the many blessings along the way are the incredible friendships around the world –borne of the size and scope of our writing community and related social media communities. And little did we realize the value of these friendships in relation to our global travels. The "norm" for us now is to add another level of planning to all our trips both domestically and internationally by exploring who we know wherever we're going –then reaching out to connect in person. With almost 1,000 writers on six continents, we've had the pleasure of migrating many of these relationships into authentic relationships.

Having just crossed over our first decade of media operations, we decided that the best way to celebrate was to finally "get off the 24/7 always-on, hamster wheel" by unplugging via a three-month "digital sabbatical" commencing later this year. Our plan is to step back, smell the roses, recharge and exhale as we rediscover each other and all else that really matters. Of all the things we do, we'll miss our weekly Friendship Bench the most, as it has become more than just a weekly Zoom call, but rather a place where real relationships happen. The kind of relationships that are hard to find these days, but priceless when discovered. We gave some thought to keeping the Friendship Bench going during our sabbatical, but with the benefit of more thought and invaluable advice, it became clear that much the same way you can't learn how to swim without jumping entirely into the water –we couldn't expect to take full advantage of the "unplugged" notion, without unplugging entirely. And as we were contemplating this final decision, we happened upon a random card sitting on the counter in a local coffee shop a while back. Printed in all caps on the card? "SELF CARE ISN'T SELFISH" ... As they say, the rest is history.

CHAPTER NINE
MORE ABUNDANCE

"ABUNDANCE MEANS THERE'S A SENSE OF POSSIBILITY. THAT THERE'S ENOUGH, AND THAT THERE'S AN EVER-EXPANDING ENOUGH."

—WHITNEY JOHNSON

"Focusing on your desired goal, keeping your why in the forefront of your thoughts and actions will automatically reveal the how."

—MARIAH EDGINGTON

Abundance. Awareness. Choice. Decisions. Those are the four words and concepts that anchor this book. There's a reason we place abundance first. Despite the flood, fire, and fury we're exposed to on cable news the world we live in is an abundant place, a much more benevolent, more compassionate and kinder world than people commonly believe. By almost every metric, the world is becoming safer, more open, better able to understand and inhabit.

Fewer people go to bed hungry today. Fewer people die in those floods, fires, and furies than have at any time in history. Life expectancy a hundred years ago worldwide was around forty years. Today, the average minimum life expectancy is forty years. Smallpox, rubella, diphtheria, tetanus, and many tropical diseases have been all but eradicated. Despite rumors of war, no states have engaged in open conflict between each other for fifty years.

More people are literate and educated than at any time. Women the world over are gaining equality, education, and their own agency and livelihoods at a steady, irreversible rate. Because of this, they're having fewer babies, and that leads to yet more educational opportunities. Far fewer cultures now inhibit girls' education, and that drives the birth rate down even further as educated girls also have fewer children. The UN estimates that by the dawn of the twenty-second century, just seventy-eight years from when this is written, the world's population will have peaked and be in decline.

The world is becoming gentler and more caring. Formerly barbaric practices like genital mutilation, the criminalization of homosexual acts, suppression of free speech, state-approved spousal rape, child labor, and sanctioned torture for open defiance of state religions is almost non-existent, and states where those barbaric practices do exist are more and more marginalized.

One hundred years ago, more than 90 percent of the world's people survived on less than a dollar a day. Today the poorest people commonly earn several times that amount, and they have cell phones, electricity, microwave ovens, washing machines, televisions, dependable transport to and from work, and access to the same venues and markets more prosperous people do. Not only is this an abundant world, it is getting more abundant by the day.

Awareness is the next word we chose. Once we become aware of the reality surrounding us, we're able to see that there are better ways and better options. When we see the opportunities in front of us, that vision expands our thinking, and a mind that's been expanded never returns to its original shape or capacity. One of the central characteristics of human beings is our curiosity, and our drive to know things. So, with an expanding awareness, we realize that we want yet more of whatever the secret sauce is that gave us that awareness in the first place. It's not a linear progression, in other words. It's a geometric one, and the first awakening—first awareness—of that is exhilarating!

Choice is next. With the possible exception of breathing and heartbeat, everything in your life is a choice. We're not being facetious. Abraham Lincoln once said, "A man is as happy as he makes up his mind to be." We believe the sixteenth president of the US was exactly right. He was simply recognizing the power of choice in our lives. We've insisted throughout this book that every decision you make, every place you go, and the way you conduct yourself every day is a choice.

Finally, Decision. We also write, in several places, that our thoughts produce our reality and our lives. That is true. But just thinking about what you desire, and taking no appropriate action, will leave you desiring on and on forever. Focus is a very good thing. Indeed, it is essential to obtaining what you want and need. But action is also needed, and in curious fashion, the more you concern yourself with the how, the longer the process takes. That sounds like a major contradiction. But focusing on your desired goal, keeping your why in the forefront of your thoughts and actions will automatically reveal the how.

"Never take your press clippings seriously,
either on the good side or the bad side."
—WHITNEY JOHNSON

We wrote *Journey Well* to assert that you are <u>More</u> than enough. Notice that the word more has no limit. No one can capture the intrinsic value of more. It would be like trying to define soon, or later, or someday. It can't be done. Soon could mean ten minutes or ten months. More water could be an ounce, a gallon, or an ocean. Once you attain the level you're destined for, reach higher still. You may get a lot of feedback and flak. That's okay. You may get press clippings and PR that are highly complementary or dismally damning. Shrug it off and keep climbing. There's an old saying, "Those who can, do; those who can't, teach." Be the one who does things and disregard those who only preach about them.

You're a powerful, limitless human being. We describe you that way for a reason. Do you truly know what your limits are? Do you understand the walls and barriers confronting you? Your paradigms seem to, until you dismiss their power. Your family, friends, and business acquaintances seem to know your limits. But they don't even know who you truly are, so how could they know that you're unlimited?

As you know, there are others who struggle with this understanding. Please reach out to someone today and let them know they, too, are <u>More</u> than enough, and allow them to borrow from *your* faith in them. You never know who you'll reach when you do this.

Find stationery and write to someone who's not expecting it. That describes a lot of people these days because the world has moved to email and away from snail mail. Whoever receives your letter will be so amazed and grateful. When they open the mailbox and see an actual letter to them inside, they'll be filled with warmth. Reading each word on the page, in longhand, they'll likely read it again and again.

Plus, the feeling you'll get by imagining them opening and reading your words will fill you with happiness. Giving these unexpected gifts to others causes a flood of the feel-good chemicals in your brain. The serenity and satisfaction that brings can last a very long time.

This, too, is part of the more-than-enough equation. Claiming your new status comes with the responsibility to elevate others, as we're attempting to do for you. Embrace that mandate. Grab hold of the opportunity and explore it to its fullest. Imagine the warm feeling of accomplishment you'll have helping others in ways that bring hope, joy, and peace to those who need it. Imagine seeing them arrive at the understanding that they, too, are more than enough. Imagine watching someone you love and cherish turn their life around and thrive because you claimed your status as more than enough. Life offers nothing better.

OUR LIVES ARE OUR CV—OUR COMPLETE VALUE

By moving forward with this, realizing that you are more than enough, you're on the path to create more than you could imagine for yourself and for people around you. You'll become the focus of energy, a model for others to follow, and that's a life-changing realization.

Our lives are our CV—our Complete Value. What we bring into the world, who we serve with kindness, compassion, gratitude, and respect, the values we share with others are the parts of life that matter most and make up our personal CV.

By sweeping out the negative mind chatter, replacing it with a message I Am More Than Enough, we take a step in the direction of all we can be.

Focus on what you *can* do. Let go of those things that weigh you down, and people who don't support all you can be. Every person reading this has value. Every person reading this is <u>More</u> than Enough. You are a worthy person. Be proud of the things you've done and know that you have more amazing things to do. List some huge goals that make you stretch and grow. Make those goals big enough that they scare you. Plan them out. Review them daily.

As our attitude toward ourselves improves, so will our relationships with others. People want to be around others with high energy and a positive, happy attitude. You can be that person. Not everything you think about yourself is true. You have the ability to take your past mistakes and review them closely and honestly. There are things you've done that you'd love a do-over for, yet the fact remains that your past is unchangeable. That said, you don't have to continue dragging it into the future. The most productive thing for you to do is learn from those mistakes, forgive yourself, harvest the good lessons, and leave the past where it belongs, behind you.

Interestingly, there is only one person who gets to occupy your brain space. That person is you. We're the only ones who can hear our inner voice. Is your inner voice today a friend or a foe? Stop the inner critic before it starts. Become aware of the negative messages you're allowing into your mind.

For many years, we internalized the negativity passed down to us from family and others. However, that was *their* truth. We just bought into their nonsense and false perceptions and made them ours. Now we look back and realize this behavior isn't just corrosive and untrue, it's also unattractive. It's all about energy. People don't gravitate to someone with low self-esteem. By acting out those traits, we pushed people away without meaning to.

Today, we need a telescope to see the unhappy version of ourselves from the past. We share kindness, compassion, gratitude, and respect with others. Thus, we get it back in return. Our lives are abundant in even more ways now.

If you incorporate these simple steps into a daily routine, and implement the exercises in the *Journey Well* guidebook, a year from now you, too, will need a telescope to see the old you. You'll begin your journey to the better, brighter world you deserve. The following personal journey is transcribed from an interview conducted with Whitney Johnson. Her fine insights centered on abundance and our shared opportunities in this new age, as she said, "An ever-expanding enough."

HERE ARE THREE IMPORTANT POINTS FROM THIS CHAPTER:

★ The way you conduct yourself every day is a choice

★ The more you concern yourself with the how, the longer the process takes.

★ Abundance means there's a sense of possibility that there's enough, and an ever-expanding enough.

ACTION STEPS:

≋ Look around and consider how much abundance the world holds. If it doesn't astonish you, try again.

≋ Write down five things your parents didn't have that you do. There's more available to us now than at any time in human history.

≋ Find a recent book on abundance and read it for yourself. Check our bibliography for suggestions.

PERSONAL JOURNEY

WHITNEY JOHNSON

A 50 Most Influential Management Thinkers, #14 Ranking, and Leadership Thinkers Top 8 Finalist, Whitney Johnson is the CEO of Disruption Advisors, a tech-enabled talent development company and an Inc. 5000 2020 fastest-growing private company in America. One of the ten leading business thinkers in the world as named by Thinkers50 in 2021, Whitney is an expert at smart growth leadership and author of *Smart Growth: How to Grow Your People to Grow Your Company,* and other titles.

Amazon: https://tinyurl.com/2p8vrdat

WHITNEY JOHNSON INTERVIEW 12.20.21

BE: What does abundance mean to you?

WJ: Abundance means there's a sense of possibility that there's enough, and that there's an ever-expanding enough.

ME: How do you share that with others?

WJ: It's a good question because most of us toggle in and out of scarcity and abundance. I can share it with other people when I'm feeling that way, and when I'm not feeling that way I think most people tend to want to grab things and hold onto them closely, as if there's not enough.

So I'd say to do the work, to be in a place of abundance as much as possible, and to make that ever more frequent, and sharing with other people, is the one thought that comes to mind.

Yesterday, I got on a Zoom call with a woman, and she was feeling overwhelmed, like many of us are during the holidays, and I was holding that space for her, just being there. The beautiful thing about it is, that morning I was feeling I didn't have enough time to get everything done. But when I took that time for her, she felt like she had enough, and when I got off the phone I felt like I had enough time. In a way, she filled my cup, because she gave me the opportunity to feel effective. When we feel we don't have enough, we feel like we can't be effective. So in that time, by holding that space for her, and allowing that conversation, I felt better.

ME: What unique way do you celebrate your own success and abundance?

WJ: One way I celebrate that success is I'll write it in my journal, and I'll share it with my family. So, validating it for myself means sharing it with someone else. In that moment, when I feel I'm being successful, something works, or someone reads a copy of the book and says this is really helpful, if I'm in an abundant place then I want to help even more.

ME: You show up, and I've learned so much from you.

WJ: And you show up for me! You participate, and you comment. It's like a virtuous cycle, so I'm grateful that you think it's helpful, and we sometimes feel like when we're talking back, even though it feels asymmetrical, the experience I'm having is not.

BE: So, let me ask you. Have you had the inner critic during your time (writing) *Smart Growth?*

WJ: Great question. I tend to not think I have imposter syndrome. One of the things that's interesting is that it shows up unawares. For example, you probably realize that when you're writing a book it's not really a solitary effort, you're writing it together. It's much more communal than anyone expects. So one thing I had to struggle with is, because I'm not writing every single word, I had other writers, I had editors. So, yes it's my book, yes it's my writing, but I also had a lot of other people writing, so I think when you're doing something in a communal way, and you put your name on it, you think, well, should my name really be there? That's an interesting thing I had to sort through, and that happens to anybody running any sort of business.

The other place it kind of crept in where I didn't expect it, the Thinkers 50 rankings came out a couple of months ago, and I ended up in the top 10. And when I got in the top 10, first of all, when my name wasn't read, I thought, well I'm not going to get in at all. Then when I got in the top 10, I thought, well, I shouldn't be there, I should be there in 2 years, not now. So I said, that's imposter syndrome, right?

I was talking to my friend Liz Wiseman, who wrote *Multipliers*. She said, Whitney, in life there are things you're going to do that you're going to be surprised that you're there, and sometimes other people are going to be surprised that you're there. The only thing that actually matters is what you do next. So, I'm here whether anybody else thinks I should be. There are times I probably should have been on the list, and times I probably shouldn't be and I am, and the question is once you're in that place, what do you do? That's how we deal with that, never taking your press clippings too seriously, either on the good side, or the bad side.

BE: In our research for *Journey Well*, we came across the fact that Albert Einstein considered himself 'an involuntary swindler,' he had imposter syndrome. So, we're all in pretty good company.

WJ: That's interesting, because, he was brilliant, it's not that he didn't think he was smart, but he had colleagues around him that were also smart, that weren't getting the accolades he was.

ME: Excellent point. So, speaking of Journeying Well, how do you journey well personally?

WJ: I would say that when I am journeying well — some days I journey well better than others — it's because I'm present. I'm in the moment. I'm living my life according to what I say I value, so according to my faith, spending time with my family, treating people with respect and dignity, making choices. All those things come together in that place where I'm feeling present, and I'm good with God. If those things are in place, then I know I'm journeying well.

BE: This sounds like awareness.

WJ: Yes. Like, right now, we're having this conversation, *right now*. Are we focused on this conversation? And the answer is yes.

ME: One last question. What did you find most valuable talking to us?

WJ: I like that discussion of abundance, when I made the connection between holding space for someone else, and then she allowed me to feel effective, that created abundance for me in an unexpected way. That was really useful. Something else. The two of you seem very calm, and that's what you're writing about, you're in a place to write about it because you're living it. That's the experience I'm having.

ME/BE: Whitney, thank you very much for your time today.

WJ: You're welcome, thank you.

CHAPTER TEN

COMPETITIVE MIND / CREATIVE MIND

"WE NEED TO BE SMARTER THAN OUR BRAINS SOMETIMES."

—DR. MELISSA HUGHES

"Your body might crave caffeine, but your brain craves serenity."
—BYRON EDGINGTON

There are many ways you can open your mind and heart and soul to vistas you never imagined. We covered a few of these in Visioneering. You can think deeply about something, taking it apart and reassembling it in your mind, imagining a whole new assembly and use for it. This works for physical as well as mental and emotional things. Doing this, you'll expand your consciousness in ways that never occurred to you. There are concepts that have been scientifically proven that will take you to a plane much higher than you ever imagined.

Some of what you'll read in this chapter of *Journey Well* might make you shake your head and wonder what we've been smoking.

We ask that you read on, keep an open mind (which will open further, as you'll see), and absorb this information like you would a chilled iced tea on a steamy summer day.

Let us explain the chapter title: To open our minds to new and different things we must suppress the so-called "competitive mind." When we're using this part of our minds, which is almost all the time as we navigate our busy, noisy, frantic world, our creative mind takes a back seat. When we remove ourselves from the cacophony of modern life, we're able to give our creativity its freedom.

When you step outside of the frantic, competitive, commercially necessary aspect of your life and silence the various outside assaults on your time and attention your ability to think, and see, and imagine return easily, allowing you to view things differently.

There's a reason you seek the quiet of a coffee shop. Your body might crave caffeine, but your brain craves serenity. At some level, it's simple physics. When you're assaulted by outside intrusions, your first instinct is to shield yourself, to protect yourself, and perhaps even get away from whatever outside noise or intrusion you're facing.

Like the rest of us, you're a highly creative person. You may deny it but think of where you've come from and where you've been. Think of the career choices, the personal choices you've made. Those choices weren't made by someone else; they were created and actualized by you. They came from your creative mind. But they were allowed to present themselves to you while your creative mind had the latitude and the opportunity to act on those choices, and to bring into being whatever creation you made.

If we've looked for something, that means we expected to find it. It's only then that we'll be able to bring it into our lives. As Bob Proctor often said, "If you can hold it in your head, you can hold it in your hand." In other words, regardless of what it is, if you imagine it existing in your life, you can own it. A new car, a new job, a bigger, better home, or tickets to the Broadway production of Hamilton. If you can think those things arriving in your life, and then take action, you can have them.

If you doubt that theory, look around. Do you live in a decent, safe, and accepting home? Were those things granted to you? Or did you imagine them, and make them happen? Do you have a career, a car, sufficient food? Those things didn't magically appear on your doorstep delivered by an Amazon Prime driver. You first created their existence, imagined that they were available to you, and they were manifested with your intentions and actions.

Is it easy to get what you want? No. It requires action on your part, obviously. It demands whatever resources you need to expend either time, or money. None of the things we mentioned arrives by itself. But you *can* obtain anything you want. That part is true.

As we mentioned in visioneering, what you focus on expands. If you hope to write a *New York Times* best-selling book, get busy writing it. Visioneer about it. Think about it like never before, and it will show up in your life. Write it down just like this: I am happy and grateful <u>now that</u> I am a *New York Times* best-selling author.

Write it twenty times every morning, and twenty times every night. Make the *New York Times* best-selling goal a part of your life. If you take action, and if you believe it's already done, it will find its way into your life, and onto the shelves at your library and bookstore.

You might refer to this exercise as hocus-pocus. But it's better described as hocus-focus. Our subconscious minds absorb whatever stories and anecdotes we feed them. They don't take in anything else, and they don't filter anything. They're magnets that absorb everything we tell them, every thought we allow.

Your subconscious mind is like a puppy: It may be the only friend you have that trusts you no matter what. It reads whatever thoughts your conscious mind is entertaining, soaks them in, and brands them indelibly into your mental iPad. The subconscious doesn't make its own thoughts, feelings, or reality. It responds to whatever the conscious mind sends it and stores it away. It cannot do otherwise because that would be beyond its purview.

The upside is this: If you feed your subconscious mind wholesome, positive fare, guess what it stores on your hard drive? That's right—wholesome, positive fare. When that happens, your world glows. It lightens up, and you revel in positive energy. Likewise, if you feed your subconscious negative, sinister, dark and foreboding fare, it happily takes that in and your world grows darker. It's a choice. Especially today, when you're immersed in dark and dismal data from social media, cable news, and various other sources of negative news, it's difficult to avoid tarnishing your subconscious and dimming the lights.

So, if you wish to claim your better, brighter world, the choice is clear: Stop absorbing all that negative energy. Turn off the constant news feed, ignore the serial poisoners on your social media feeds, and gravitate toward positive, uplifting sites.

What's this got to do with your NYT best seller? It takes the same kind of focus and energy as your attention to other things. What you focus on expands. Here are principles that can be used to change your mind, literally.

1—Act as if: In other words, believe you are a best-selling author. Imagine yourself at a book signing, with people lined up across the bookstore holding your *New York Times* best-selling book, waiting with their pens poised for you, the successful author, to sign their copy.

2—Get uncomfortable: Counterintuitive? Perhaps, but doing the same thing you've always done gives you the same results you always got. How could it be otherwise? Take a bold, forceful, terrifying leap and trust that you'll land exactly where you wanted to. You've likely heard that life begins outside your comfort zone. So does unimagined success.

3—Dream big: You can never go beyond your own imagined capacities. No one ever succeeded beyond their stated goal regardless how grandiose that goal was. So, imagine bigger, better, more expensive, and more exciting. Leave no room for doubt. As Price Pritchett Ph.D. writes in *You²* "If you must doubt something, doubt your limits."

4—<u>Self-Assess:</u> Discern what your paradigms are because they dictate what you think, and what you do. Our paradigms are the autopilots of our lives. They use the same data stored in your subconscious to supply the reactions you have to every stimulus. When you sneered at the statement about being a best-selling author, automatically dismissing the possibility, that was your paradigm in action telling you it will never happen. This can be hard, discouraging work. But uncovering your limiting paradigms can be the most liberating exercise you ever do.

5—<u>Obey the law:</u> Recognize the binary law of the universe. For every up there must be a down; for every in, there's an out; with every high, there's a low. Once you assimilate this law into your thoughts, understanding that it must be true, your default to positive and successful becomes automatic. Henry Ford once said, "If you think you can, or if you think you can't, either way you're right!" That binary proposition from Mr. Ford cannot be otherwise.

6—<u>Your choice:</u> You are in charge of your thoughts. No one else. Victor Frankl spent years in a Nazi concentration camp. His beloved book, *Man's Search for Meaning* includes his most enduring lesson: "There's a space between every situation and your response to it. In that space lies your power to choose." Only you can choose how you react to what happens around you.

7—Decide what you want: The reason most people don't get what they want is because they don't know what it is. By deciding what you want, making it exquisitely clear to the universe in minute detail, you will usher it into your life. That's why it's critical that you see the autograph seekers holding your book, watching them smile as you take it from them to sign, and thanking them for buying your best seller.

8—Mirror, mirror: Self-image drives all else. When you look in the mirror each morning and see a happy, successful, smiling person looking back your day is already energized and awaiting the newest captured goal. The mirror work we mention in the book and the guidebook gets you to that point if it's done on a regular basis. It may seem awkward at first but do it consistently and it will change your life.

9—No *How:* Drop the phrase "how will I do that?" from your vocabulary. This may sound woo-woo and make you sneer again but dwelling on the "how" part of your goal prods you back into your competitive mind and away from your creative mind. You'll find yourself competing against the "no way," and the "you wish," and the "never happen," and you already know that those thoughts are deal breakers. Focus on your goal, forget the how, embrace the why, and use all your energy going forward.

10—<u>Listen to your heart:</u> Ignore the naysayers, and those who try to bring you down. Here's the personal aspect of this exercise. Any time you step outside your tribal position, your social network, and aim higher than you've gone before, you will get resistance. Friends, family, children, work colleagues will notice the change, and their reaction could be confusion, antagonism, or fascination. This is entirely normal. We're tribal creatures. When we step outside our group, leave the comfort and safety of the circled wagons, and set forth on a grand adventure, the response of others can cover a range of human emotions. Ignore that. It demands focus as well. It's your goal, not theirs. Just remember to wave as you drive away in your new red Toyota.

HERE ARE THREE IMPORTANT POINTS FROM THIS CHAPTER:

★ Everything is a choice. You're in charge of your thoughts, and no one can force you to think something.

★ Focus on the positives in your life and avoid the negatives. What you feed your subconscious creates your world.

★ Dream big. You will never attain anything that's beyond your aspiration, no matter how high that aspiration is.

ACTION STEPS:

≋ Begin ushering things you want into your life, things like *New York Times* best-selling books and bright red Toyotas.

≋ Start journaling about them. Do it twice a day, both morning and evening. Write "I am happy and grateful <u>now that</u>..."

≋ Write down whatever you desire most. Keep your focus there and take action to bring it into your life.

≋ Think "from the end," in other words, as if those things already exist in your life. Then act accordingly.

PERSONAL JOURNEY
ZEN BENEFIEL & MELISSA HUGHES

This Personal Journey comes from an episode of the podcast One World in a New World which aired November ninth 2021. Zen Benefiel is a Featured Author at BIZCATALYST 360° and the podcast host.

Melissa Hughes Ph.D. is State Program Director at Give Back, published author, TEDx Speaker, self-claimed Neuroscience Geek, and contributor at BIZCATALYST 360°.

Zen Benefiel (ZB) hosts the podcast, and his guest Dr. Melissa Hughes Ph.D. (MH) share a conversation about our brains, connections, mirror neurons, why positive focus is critical, the science of empathy and awe, and how humans differ from potato bugs.

⌒

MH: We have a sense of empathy. We know what it feels like for somebody else having a terrible, horrible day. Because of sensing that empathy, I'm generating those stress hormones in *their* brain. So, knowing I'm responsible for negative neurochemistry in somebody else's brain, we share the human connection.

When you make eye contact with somebody who's smiling at you, it's impossible not to smile back. That's our mirror neurons at work. When we pass each other, smile, and make eye contact, *your* brain is going to produce those good, happy chemicals in *my* brain. That empathy is part of what separates us from potato bugs and other life forms.

I'll give you 3 practical strategies. One, what you communicate on the outside of your body impacts what happens on the *inside* of somebody else's body. Two, diaphragmatic breathing is the best way to tell your body I'm OK. Today we don't have to be on the lookout for the saber tooth tiger, but there are times when our survival brain is engaged when it doesn't have to be.

ZB: I include putting your fingertips together, feeling your heartbeat. It calms you, and gets you out of your head, and into your heart.

MH: The third thing is so simple it's often forgotten and that's gratitude. When we express gratitude to another human being, we get a greater neurological benefit from that than the recipient of that gratitude.

ZB: That's the essence of namaste!

MH: Absolutely! So, challenge yourself every Friday, or whatever the end of your workweek is, get a thank you card. It could be for a coworker, a neighbor, doesn't matter. Sit down, write it out, tell them why you appreciate them. What it does is reinforce why their action was meaningful to you!

ZB: We engage in this kind of behavior that you can use over and over, and it will take you to some unimaginable heights!

MH: I get that not everybody cares about what's going on between their ears the way I do. But when you really understand these things, and what a profound impact it has on your cognition, you know that it influences everything.

ZB: From a quantum physics perspective, in this physicality we're 99% space, so...perhaps there's a greater consciousness that's in that space that's managing things just looking for opportunity to show up in our lives.

MH: There's been a lot of work done in science right now on the concept of awe, and why we need to experience the awesome things in the world. There are two ways to look at it, being so small in this universe that is so amazing, so vast, with so many unknowns. On one hand you can say I'm so small I can't make a difference. But on the other hand, it makes us realize how amazing life is, and how amazing our brains are, how amazing our relationships and how important it is to embrace that human connection, even if it's just a blip on the screen of our day. You never know how important it's going to be for that other person. Everybody's fighting a battle you know nothing about.

Remember that. A random smile can be the difference in another person's day.

John Lubbock summed this up in a quote: Pay attention to what you pay attention to! We find mostly what we're looking for. If you pay attention to all the negative people, places, and things, then you're going to find negative people, places, and things! Pay attention to the positive people, places, and things, and that's what you're going to find. A brain is a busy place.

ZB: On our honeymoon in Cancun, we were in Tulum, near Chichen Itza, and we we're talking about self-awareness and all the indicators of it. We were going down a jungle road, and in a clearing were two signs— in English! They said, 'observe your intentions' and 'observe your distractions.'

MH: I really like that. We need to be smarter than our brains sometimes.

ZB: It's all about sharing different perspectives, realizing we're saying the same things from different perspectives. Thank you so much, Melissa, I appreciate your time and your attention and your intention and the interaction, it's been very special thank you, namaste!

MH: Zen, it was a pleasure.

CHAPTER ELEVEN

CELEBRATE YOU

LIFE IS A CELEBRATION.

YOU BELONG AT THIS FEAST

"The most exciting and energizing part is that by sharing your gift,
you're helping to usher this new world into reality."
—MARIAH EDGINGTON

Before you read the final chapter of *Journey Well, You Are More Than Enough* we'd like to acknowledge the hard work you've done. By reading *Journey Well,* and being open to its message, you've proven our assumption: You are indeed a child of the universe, a vital human being with much value, and a gift to share with the rest of us. Especially now when the world is struggling through a transition, and people are yearning for the amazing society we know awaits us, you're helping the transition along. No less than the trees and the stars, we all have a right to be here.

As we wrote in the introduction, your life is the most important journey you'll ever take. You owe it to yourself to make it the most exciting, fulfilling, magical, and wondrous journey it can be. You owe it to yourself to journey well.

We want to remind you that, as we're doing, you must pass this information along. You must serve others in whatever capacity you can. None of us are immune to this mandate. Giving = Receiving and giving all means receiving all you'll ever need.

Let's celebrate the new you! You've discarded old, tired luggage that's held you back, preventing you from realizing the better, brighter life you always knew was out there calling to you. You've studied the paradigms that have been steering your life, the autopilot that takes over and flies your plane, even if it's taking you in the wrong direction. You've packed all your baggage, chosen what has value and what doesn't and you've physically or emotionally burned it or used it as a stepping stone so it no longer tethers you.

THE TRUTH YOU ARE AFRAID TO SAY, IS THE TRUTH YOU MUST SAY

You understand the value and imprinting of words, and how your life and happiness are crafted by the words you choose, by not only what you say but what you tell yourself. You understand that those words have real power, so they must be chosen and used with great care. If Rev. Martin Luther King Jr. had said, "I sure wish my children could," or "I don't know about my kids and their future," his message would have been diluted and lost to history. But when he stated, "I have a dream!" people hungry for his powerful message rallied to it. Taking his words to heart, we dreamed of the same world Dr. King did, a world where our children would be judged "Not by the color of their skin, but by the content of their character!"

The powerful words Dr. King used that long ago August day moved the world. Words do that. You understand that, so your positive, uplifting words, especially used with yourself going forward will reflect that understanding.

IT DOESN'T MATTER WHO YOU ARE, OR WHO YOUR PARENTS ARE, WHAT MATTERS IS HOW YOU THINK ABOUT WHO YOU ARE

You're a lot more familiar now with so-called impostor syndrome, and how the lack of confidence it shamelessly peddles can hinder your progress regardless of how much expertise, experience, or credentialing you may have. You know how to defeat the judgmental voice in your head. You know how to banish those useless messages and proceed with full confidence in whatever endeavor you choose.

You know that failure can be a very good thing, that *failing forward* is one certain way to confront and defeat imposter syndrome, rendering it irrelevant. The more comfortable you get with failure, knowing it always takes you closer to your goal, the more diminished and distant is the obnoxious roommate's raspy and useless voice. This is reperception, your ability to look at things, including failure with fresh eyes and see the lessons provided. The Apollo astronauts "failed their way to the moon" and so can you.

You know how to take the missteps and mistakes of your past and use them to strengthen yourself going forward. It's no shame or disability to have been wisely wounded in life. It can be the biggest source of your wisdom and strength.

You know how to establish boundaries between yourself and others, especially emotional boundaries against people who refuse to honor your agency and dignity. By recognizing your value to yourself and the rest of us, you now see those dismissive, sometimes hateful people for who they are, frightened, insecure people who feel, for whatever reason, the need to bring you down, to deflect attention away from their own insecurities and fears.

The irony of it is that they're the ones who would most benefit from *your* newfound strength. You now know how to interact with them. And you know your boundaries facilitate that interaction by shielding you from the unneeded chaff and chaos of *their* lives. This is a critical lesson, the necessity of keeping negative, hurtful people at arm's length.

DON'T STRUGGLE SO HARD TO FIT IN. EMBRACE THE REAL YOU

You know what value to put on your own sense of place and purpose. That whatever you choose to call the powerful entity that we're immersed in—God, Allah, Elohim, Krishna, Rama, or Universal energy—you are a precious child of the entity surrounding us. You *are* here for a reason. Part of it is to serve others in some way. You know as we do that recognizing your ego and removing it from occasions to serve and give is the certain path to a rich, rewarding life.

You know how to repereceive whatever missteps and embarrassments have haunted you, turning those events and behaviors around to see them as an important step taking you to this time and place. You understand that it's too easy to stay in those times, even if you can't stay in those places. Entering this new world matches up the new time and place, allowing you to breathe the fresh, clear air of this promising new day.

You're much more familiar with the precepts, and the necessity, of self-care, and how taking care of your own physical, emotional, and spiritual well-being facilitates the rest of your journey. You understand in your heart and soul that receiving means giving, and that giving to yourself is critical too. You can't share from an empty cup.

You understand the vital skill of visioneering in crafting your wonderful life. If you can hold it in your head, you can hold it in your hand. You've looked around, seen all the things you once imagined. They have now come to you, so you trust that process. You're excited and humbled. Excited because you realize visioneering will bring whatever you imagine into your life, and humbled because you feel the universe working through you to make it happen.

Of course, it's humbling. Sensing such astonishing power, and knowing you're working alongside it, is nothing short of miraculous. Don't be afraid of it. You also know that this universal energy is more benevolent than you ever imagined. Give in to it and get comfortable with it.

RE-YOU-ABLE ENERGY™ IS THE POWER
THAT COMES FROM BEING YOU

You understand that you have a precious gift that's unique to you, that billions of people have a gift as well, and all our gifts are different. This realization is even more astonishing. You're now able to imagine the bright, generous, loving, and gentle world that awaits you, a world that's not only beautiful and better, but a world that is possible. And the most exciting and energizing part is that by sharing your gift, you're helping to usher this new world into reality.

You know in your heart and soul that you are More than enough. That your place in this universe is entirely justified, and perfectly sensible, and that you're here for a reason. You're able to imagine the reality of that statement, that you're here on purpose, and that purpose is to bring whatever unique gift you hold in your heart to the world, and the sooner the better. And it is a choice. Only if you believe in your heart and soul that it can happen for you will it happen. You attract what you are. Live your life as the class act that you're working to become. When you do believe abundance will flood your life with all good things. As Kim Calvert of Dynamite Lifestyle says, "Believe in your ability to create an abundant lifestyle. You will never go beyond that which you believe."

You're on a wonderful journey, a voyage of discovery unlike any you've ever made. This journey takes you places and shows you things you may never have expected. You understand that welcoming these things into your life is no longer fearful or strange. There are no mistakes. You know when things, experiences, and people appear at just the right time, and not a minute too soon or late, that you've arrived where you need to be.

WRAPPING UP—
YOUR GIFT

Thank you for reading *Journey Well, You Are <u>More</u> Than Enough.* Thank you as well for claiming your own value. We hope you enjoyed our book, and that you find much value in it.

Thank you for sharing your gift with our world, and for being the powerful human being you are and always were. We intend for you all good things: a great life, good health, beautiful friendships, the purest love, the brightest days, the most peaceful of nights.

Here's what we ask. Become the best version of you. Do it through introspection, reflection, reperception, and repetition. Build up the vibrant person that's buried under years of false paradigms and assumptions. Do it with mirror work, and the "I AM" exercise. Claim it using the four anchor words in this book: Abundance, Awareness, Choices, and Decisions.

You're an extraordinary individual with so much to bring to the rest of us. What's hiding inside astonishes and moves you. It lights you up and *lightens* you up. It ignites the fire within that's remained dim and just out of reach, the astonishing glow of the amazing person you know has been there all along. It allows you to...

Journey Well,

Because

You Are <u>More</u> Than Enough!

ACKNOWLEDGMENTS

We wish to acknowledge all those who helped shape this book and who ushered it into being. First, our dear friends, our contributors. Your personal journeys strengthened *Journey Well* beyond measure. Thank you so much for sharing them. In order of the additions: Cathy Griffin for your brave and wonderful piece, Ahmad Imam, TM, Kim Calvert, Cory Warfield, Rachel Beck, Diane Wyzga, Laura Staley Ph.D, Brad Burchnell, Ali & Dennis Pitocco, Zen Benefiel, Melissa Hughes Ph.D, and Whitney Johnson. To Jared Kuritz at Strategies PR, Cindy Doty amazing proofer, and Jeremy Taylor our designer par excellence, many thanks for your expertise.

To our LinkedIn tribe, the extremely generous and competent people we interact with daily, you've taught us so much about goodness, abundance, gratitude, and awareness. These are the focal points of *Journey Well, You Are More Than Enough.*

To those who reached back when we reached out, many thanks, we appreciate your time and invaluable insight.

To those we failed to mention, know that we recognize your place in our abundance.

Thank you all, Journey Well!
(Re)Discover Your Passion, Purpose,
Your Love of Yourself and Life!

ABOUT THE AUTHORS

Mariah and Byron Edgington wrote *Journey Well, You Are More Than Enough* as a challenge to everyone to attain the kinds of relationships and lives that bring peace and serenity, and to build lives that matter. Mariah and Byron have three beautiful daughters and six grandchildren. They live and write in Iowa City Iowa. Contact them through their website:

www.mariahedgington.com.

Access the *Journey Well* guidebook at the author website. The *Journey Well* online course is also available at their website, or through Udemy.

After reading *Journey Well You Are More Than Enough:* to give back and show your appreciation, please:

- Write a book review on Amazon, Goodreads or both.
- Gift a copy of *Journey Well* to someone else or your library.
- Share info about *Journey Well* on social media.
- Share a photo of the book's cover on Instagram & Pinterest.
- Share *Journey Well* with your book club.
- Mention *Journey Well* on a blog or podcast.

To connect with the authors:

- Contact us for an interview.
- Contact us for live readings/signings.
- Contact us for bulk orders.
- Join the *Journey Well* Facebook group.
- Read & review other authors' works listed in the bibliography.

To continue your journey:

- Download the *Journey Well* guidebook.
- Enjoy the *Journey Well* online course through the website or Udemy.
- Connect with and support our contributors and affiliates.

Please use the following hashtags for *Journey Well*:

#journeywellyouaremorethanenough

#journeywell

#morethanenough

#reyouableenergy

Thank you, and Journey Well,

Mariah and Byron Edgington

OUR CONTRIBUTORS
(WITH GRATITUDE AND LOVE)

Rachel Beck: linkedin.com/in/vlakshmiauthor

Zen Benefiel: linkedin.com/in/zenbenefiel

Brad Burchnell: linkedin.com/in/bradburchnell

Kim Calvert: linkedin.com/in/kim-calvert-b68416213

Cathy Griffin: linkedin.com/in/cathy-griffin1

Dr. Melissa Hughes: linkedin.com/in/melissahughesphd

Ahmad Imam: linkedin.com/in/theahmadimam

Whitney Johnson: linkedin.com/in/whitneyjohnson/

TM: We hope your world is better, and brighter. All the best to you and please let us know how you are.

Ali and Dennis Pitocco: linkedin.com/in/dennisjpitocco

Laura Staley: linkedin.com/in/laurastaley1

Cory Warfield: linkedin.com/in/corywarfield

Diane Wyzga: linkedin.com/in/diane-f-wyzga-qmsa

BIBLIOGRAPHY

Abundant Heart, Thoughts on Healing, Loving, and Living Free ©2021 Laura Staley
As a Man Thinketh: Original 1902 edition ©2020 James Allen
Awakened Imagination ©1954 Neville (Goddard)
Change Your Paradigm, Change Your Life ©2021 Bob Proctor
Dusk, Night, Dawn ©2021 Anne LaMott
Finding Your Way When Life Changes Your Plans ©2018 V. Lakshmi
Gratitude Heals ©2019 Linda Roszak Burton
Happy-ier Hour with Einstein ©2018 Dr. Melissa Hughes
Love Wins ©2016 Jim Obergefell and Debbie Cenziper
Mirror Work ©2016 Louise Hay
10 Secrets for Success and Inner Peace ©2001 Wayne W. Dyer
The Power of Intention ©2004 Wayne W. Dyer
The Go Giver ©2007 Bob Burg & John David Mann
The Hill We Climb 2021 Amanda Gorman
The Power of Awareness ©1952 Neville (Goddard)
Think and Grow Rich ©1937 Napoleon Hill
This Taste of Flesh and Bones ©2019 R. Arthur Russell
Thrive ©2014, 2015 Christabella LLC Arianna Huffington
The Sleep Revolution ©2016, 2017 Christabella LLC Arianna Huffington
The Success Principles ©2005 Jack Canfield
The 5 Buckets ©2021 Bobby Dysart
Psycho-Cybernetics ©Maxwell Maltz MD, FICS
You² ©2012 Price Pritchett
You Can Heal Your Life ©1984 Louise Hay
Your Invisible Power ©2013(?) Genevieve Behrend
Your Time to Thrive ©2021 Marina Khidekel, and Editors of Thrive Global

OTHER BOOKS BY BYRON EDGINGTON ATP, CRMI

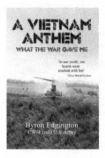

A Vietnam Anthem describes what effects the war in SouthEast Asia had on its author, and the man he became afterward, both good and bad. The war in Vietnam was a national tragedy. The author carries a lot of ambivalence about it, because, as horrible as his participation in the war was, it gave him a gratifying career in commercial aviation.

https://tinyurl.com/y6uzftyz

The Sky Behind Me, a Memoir of Flying and Life is the author's personal recollections of a life in the sky, and his memories from the cockpit. For forty years the author flew helicopters all over the world, both commercially and in the military. He doused forest fires in Alaska, counted power poles in Ohio, reported news and traffic in several large American cities, and for twenty years he rescued ill and injured medical patients while based at a hospital in Iowa. TSBM details a life lived in the generous, beautiful, always challenging, and often dangerous sky.

https://tinyurl.com/5du4r8na

Waiting for Willie Pete is a helicopter novel of Vietnam. Based on *Moby Dick*, *Waiting for Willie Pete* is a tale of desperation, obsession, danger, and the vicissitudes of war. Filled with Melvillean characters modeled on men the author flew with in combat—Captain A'Hearn, Piper, Starkey, Stebbins, Fisk, and more, it's a stark portrayal of what the Vietnam war was truly like, especially for helicopter crews. As Sergeant Quillig says, 'war is not on fields of battle; war is in the minds and hearts of men.'

https://tinyurl.com/ww5dc

PostFlight: An Old Pilot's Logbook is a memoir/self-help book written for young, aspiring pilots. In the author's words, "*PostFlight* is full of valuable information I wish I'd had when I started flying 50 years ago." Full of personal tales, close calls, interactions with other pilots, passengers, mechanics, and employers in the flying business, *PostFlight* is a resource for anyone who dreams of a life in the cockpit, especially young women. *PostFlight: An Old Pilot's Logbook.*

https://tinyurl.com/mryp9vmu

ALL BOOKS ARE AVAILABLE ON AMAZON, OR
THROUGH THE AUTHORS' WEBSITES:

www.mariahedgington.com
www.byronedgington.com

CPSIA information can be obtained
at www.ICGtesting.com
Printed in the USA
BVHW050453170722
641899BV00002B/158